SOMERSET
DRAGONS

this book is

dedicated

To

all those

Dragons and Knights

that have given so much pleasure

SOMERSET DRAGONS

Brian Wright

To save a maid, St George a dragon slew,
A pretty tale, if all that's told be true.
Most say there are no dragons; and 'tis said
There was no George. Pray God there was a maid!

Anonymous
Quoted by John Aubrey in the
late seventeenth century

TEMPUS

First published 2002

PUBLISHED IN THE UNITED KINGDOM BY:
Tempus Publishing Ltd
The Mill, Brimscombe Port
Stroud, Gloucestershire GL5 2QG

PUBLISHED IN THE UNITED STATES OF AMERICA BY:
Tempus Publishing Inc.
2 Cumberland Street
Charleston, SC 29401
USA

British Library Cataloguing in Publication Data.
A catalogue record for this book is available from the British Library.

ISBN 0 7524 2606 0

Typesetting and origination by Tempus Publishing.
PRINTED AND BOUND IN GREAT BRITAIN.

CONTENTS

A medieval corbel in Wells Cathedral with a crocodile-like carving - perhaps the inspiration for some early dragon imagery.

Introduction

For centuries, indeed thousands of years, man's imagination has been fired by tales of dragons and the heroes who battled against them. Stories featuring dragons are found all over the world and they have been credited with all sorts of powers, attributes and characteristics. Britain is a country that is rich in dragon lore, more than ninety towns, villages and other locations having a tradition of a local dragon; or having evidence that such a story existed in the past. Among the counties of England, Scotland and Wales, Somerset seems to have more dragon legends and various items of 'evidence' than most other counties, and has even adopted the dragon as the emblem on its coat of arms. Only Yorkshire exceeds its stories by two, but with a lot less 'evidence'.

Dragon stories passed down through the generations by word of mouth and, as one would expect with an oral tradition, details changed with the retelling, names got added or lost, words changed their meaning and elements of other stories crept in. However, many of these tales survived the centuries in this form until recorded by folklore historians, usually in the late nineteenth or early twentieth century. Undoubtedly there were other dragon tales forgotten and never written down, now lost to us for ever.

The dragons of Somerset show almost the complete range of types, characteristics, habitats and profession of their slayers and represent a good overall spread of British dragon legend. In the fifteenth and sixteenth centuries, Somerset grew rich from the profits of the woollen industry and could afford to build impressive churches and employ skilled carvers of stone and wood to decorate them. The carvings illustrate many aspects of both religious belief and daily life including local legends and superstitions, some of which incorporate dragons in one form or another. Sometimes a dragon legend has been preserved in the locality, but in other cases a very specific representation of a dragon exists but no story is now known. When there is a dragon and no story, it is not unreasonable to suppose that in at least some cases, such a legend did once exist and was known at the time but has now been lost to us. Some of these fascinating carvings have been included, with a description of the scene, as they throw some light on the ideas and beliefs of these long gone inhabitants of the county. Such things as the tomb of a forgotten knight or a weather vane on a church tower, may have proved the inspiration for dragon stories to satisfy the curiosity of people in the vicinity and the opportunity to create an exciting and wondrous tale to liven up the humdrum lives of people living in a very rural county.

Sometimes more than one version of a story exists, and this too is not surprising, as several people in a district would sometimes claim to know the 'truth' about a legend. Many stories have a local setting and mention local features that would be very familiar to their listeners. Often story-tellers would end their tale with an exhortation to go and look at something to verify the truth of their tale. This might be a carving on a tomb or bench end in the local church, a spot where plants did not grow in the locality and where, it was claimed, the dragons blood was spilt or perhaps some other local feature, such as notches on the side of a hill caused by the dragon wrapping its tail around it. Pointing out such bits of 'evidence' gave a good finish to the story and reinforced the local connection with a heroic deed which, of course, was worthy of remembering as part of village 'history'.

There are representations of dragons in Somerset covering a period of twelve hundred years from the eighth or ninth century to the twentieth. They come in all forms from a Saxon carving of a dragon being slain to a design on a modern lamp-post. Many of these are to be found in or on churches where they performed a range of functions from frightening off 'evil spirits' in the case of Hunky Punk dragons, to illustrating local legends or the lives of saints who were involved with dragons; or are purely decorative elements that allowed the craftsman who created them to give full reign to his imagination. Lots of examples of Somerset dragons are featured in this book demonstrating the wide range of forms and materials in which images of dragons in Somerset have been produced but I don't claim that this is a complete guide to all the dragons in Somerset. There are still surprises awaiting Dragon Hunters who keep their eyes open while travelling in the county.

So for a while, suspend disbelief and enjoy these stories and bits of 'evidence' that have been passed down to us by generations of Somerset folk. Legends that come from a time when strange and wondrous creatures might still have lurked in the thick woodlands or those mysterious marshes, so often covered in swirling mists, when anyone with half an imagination would have found it easy to believe the storytellers.

Brian Wright
June 2002

1

The Origins of the Dragon

There are many theories concerning the origin of the dragon. Dragons have played a part in myths from all over the world, and some concern the formation of the Universe including two of the earliest of mankind's myths; the *Enuma Elish* of the Babylonians and the Hindu *Rg Veda,* which feature such creatures. A traditional north European creation myth also features dragons:

At the dawn of time only a yawning abyss stretched through space. Eventually, water appeared, and from this the land emerged. Then the first human was created, and this was the giant Ymir, who alone gave birth to man and woman. From these several generations of giants and humans were born and multiplied until the whole universe was populated.

The universe had, at its centre, a huge ash tree called Yggdrasil, that supported nine realms, that of the gods, elves, dwarves, humans, the dead and so on. Yggdrasil had three roots that reached into the worlds of Asgard where dwelt the gods, each in his own mansion; Midgard, where man lived and Niflheim, which was the underworld where the dead would go. Niflheim was the dwelling place of the first of all the Nordic dragons, Nidhoggr - 'the dread biter', who spent his time gnawing at the root of the universal tree in an attempt to destroy it.

In this task he was assisted by several lesser dragons and serpents. However, his efforts to destroy the tree were in vain, as beings called Norns repaired the tree each day by sprinkling it with gravel, and then watering it from a sacred well.

It was said the most serious threat to Yggdrasil would be at the End of the World, but even then the tree would survive. Nidhoggr would finally accept he was thwarted in his task and would fly off over the hills of darkness and bear away the bodies of the dead on his wings.

This story was later given a modified Christian significance, and a number of Norman church carvings around the country depict the Tree of Life being devoured by one or two dragons, usually found on the tympana, the curved area above the main door into the building. In the standard version of the Bible we are told there was the Tree of Life and the Tree of the Knowledge of Good and Evil. The second tree was expressly forbidden to man and is the one shown in pictorial representations of the Fall. Man was told he could eat of any other tree in the garden, so he had the opportunity of eating of the Tree of Life and so gaining immortality. However, the 'serpent' persuaded him to eat of the Tree of Knowledge, upon which he was banished from the Garden of Eden and so lost the opportunity to gain immortality by eating of the Tree of Life.

The words 'serpent' and 'dragon' are often interchangeable in biblical translations and the Norman carvings of this scene often feature a dragon or dragons near the tree or eating it, a symbolic scene reminding all those who are about to enter the church that only by keeping faithful to God could they hope for their souls to gain immortality, and evil was always lurking nearby to put temptation in their way and so destroy their immortal life. The serpent in the Garden of Eden is sometimes shown as a dragon in early paintings and prints. After the fruit of the tree has been eaten it says in *Genesis* 3.14 :

> And the Lord God said unto the serpent, Because thou hast done this, thou art cursed above all cattle, and above every beast of the field; upon thy belly shalt thou go, and dust shalt thou eat all the days of thy life.

As a serpent already goes upon its belly the curse would be meaningless unless it already had legs that the Lord deprived it of - in which case it started life as a dragon!

Somerset's best example of a Tree of Life carving features a griffin and another creature rather than dragons, although a possible Tree of Life and dragon may be featured on the Norman font at Isle Abbots church.

Dragons also appear in the myths of ancient Greece, and indeed the word 'dragon' is derived from the Greek 'drakon' which also includes snakes of many types, both real and mythological. From this is derived the Anglo-Saxon words which in turn have given rise to 'drake' used as a dialect word for dragon in some parts of Britain.

There are references to dragons in the Bible, in both the Old and New Testaments, and while such examples no doubt fired the imaginations of

Eve and the Serpent. A woodcut by Gunther Zainer (1470) showing a dragon-like serpent.

the superstitious people of Somerset who heard them, descriptions of dragons as they are appear in the Bible, seem to have played little part in the way dragons were depicted in the county, either in the churches or other places. However, the idea of dragons passed into the Christian mythology of the medieval period. In both the Old and the New Testaments dragons are used to represent evil in general, and sometimes the Devil specifically, as in the story of St Michael as it appears in the Book of the Revelation of St John (see below).

Even at this early date more than one type of dragon was recognized. There are various references to 'Leviathan', which literally means 'coiled', and is distinguished from another type, 'Rahab', which means the 'defiant'.

Versions of the Bible use different words for these creatures, more recent editions tend to use the word serpent or asp, while earlier ones use the term dragon. In the Vulgate Bible, compiled by St Jerome over a fifteen-year period at the request of Pope Damasus in 382, the term dragon is very common, and it was the Vulgate Bible that became the first printed version - the Gutenburg Bible of 1456. In this even 'Leviathan' is rendered as 'draco' - dragon. The English 1611 version of the Bible includes more 'dragons' than later versions. In the Old Testament dragons are mentioned many times, but are not described in detail and most of them live in the sea. Sometimes references to 'dragon' and 'leviathan' co-exist. Here are a few examples:

Their wine is the poison of dragons and the cruel venom of asps.'
Deuteronomy 32:33

Am I the monster of the deep, am I the sea-serpent, that thou settest a watch over me?
Job 7:12

With his strong arm he cleft the sea-monster, and struck down the Rahab by his skill.
Job 26:12

Thou didst divide the sea by thy strength: thou brakest the heads of the dragons in the waters.

Thou brakest the heads of Leviathan in pieces, and gavest him to be meat to the people inhabiting the wilderness.
Psalms 74:13-14

Thou shalt tread upon the lion and serpent: the young lion and the dragon shalt thou trample under feet.
Psalms 91:13

In that day the Lord with his sore and great and strong sword shall punish leviathan and the piercing serpent, even leviathan that crooked serpent; and he shall slay the dragon that is in the sea.
Isaiah 27:1

And thorns shall come up in her palaces, nettles and brambles in the fortresses thereof: And it shall be an habitation of dragons, and a court of owls.
Isaiah 34:13

Was it not you who healed the Rahab in pieces and ran the dragon through?
Isaiah 51:9

They hatch cockatrice eggs, and weave the spiders web: he that eateth of their eggs dieth, and that which is crushed breaketh out into a viper.
Isaiah 59:5

For, behold, I will send serpents, cockatrices, among you, which will not be charmed, and they shall bite you, saith the Lord.

Jeremiah 8:17)

In the New Testament dragons are sometimes described in a little more detail, a notable example appearing in the Book of the Revelation of St John:

And there appeared another wonder in heaven; and behold a great red dragon, having seven heads and ten horns, and seven crowns upon his heads.

And his tail drew the third part of the stars of heaven, and did cast them to the earth: and the dragon stood before the woman which was ready to be delivered, for to devour her child as soon as it was born.

Revelation 12:3-4

St. John also describes the actions of St Michael, a dragon-fighting saint, to whom a number of Somerset churches have been dedicated. In this case the dragon is Satan:

And then there was war in Heaven: Michael and his angels fought against the dragon; and the dragon fought and his angels, and prevailed not; neither was their place found any more in heaven.

And the great dragon was cast out, that old serpent, called the Devil, and Satan, which deceiveth the whole world: he was cast out into the earth, and his angels were cast out with him.

Revelation 12:7-9

And I saw an angel come down from heaven, having the key of the bottomless pit and a great chain in his hand.
And he laid hold on the dragon, that old serpent, which is the Devil and Satan, and bound him a thousand years.

Revelation 20:1-2

Other references to dragons indicate they were regarded as the mouth-pieces of Satan, and later were regarded as bringing forth evil:

Then I saw coming from the mouth of the dragon, the mouth of the beast, and the mouth of the false prophet, three foul spirits like frogs.

These spirits were devils, with power to work miracles.

Revelation 16:13-14

The use of dragon imagery could also represent the victory of Christianity over paganism and so was a suitably dangerous and appropriate foe for a saintly hero to fight. In this role saints and dragons appear as carvings in a number of Somerset churches, often as war memorials. Dragon stories attached to the lives and adventures of Christian saints often appear to be symbolic of holiness overcoming evil, the Devil or paganism, or all three.

When carved on a church font the dragon symbolized the Devil and so a child was freed when it was baptized from the 'danger' into which it had been born and prepared for its own personal fight against the evil in the world.

A number of dragons are to be found on some of the very fine medieval carved bench ends in Somerset churches. The types of dragons shown were probably influenced by representations in medieval Bestiaries, books that gave moral instruction from the supposed habits of both real animals and fabulous beasts. The inspiration for many of these medieval books and encyclopaedias was *Physiologus* – 'a discourse on nature', probably written in the third century and consisting of a collection of strange tales about real and imaginary animals for use in moral instruction. *Physiologus* is first mentioned in the fifth century and was pronounced heretical a century later. In the eleventh century the scholar, Theobald, Abbot of Monte Cassino from 1022-35, arranged the information under headings of beasts, birds and fishes and it was largely his accounts that were used as the basis for medieval works involving animal symbolism in literature and art, including carvings that appeared in and on churches. The complex underlying symbolism described in these works, well understood at the time, explains some of the more unusual dragon 'scenes' featured.

Many of the British dragon legends incorporate some elements of the classical myths. The original hero of the story, Herakles, Perseus or Jason becomes replaced by a local hero. Classical myths became known in Britain during the early medieval period and the profile of the dragon was raised even further from the twelfth century when the story of St George and his adventures with a dragon was brought back by crusader knights. Once St George had been adopted as England's patron saint in 1222 the idea of dragons became more widespread.

The imagery and representations of the dragon was used to symbolize many things, and examples of most of them can be found in Somerset in one form or another. The early dragons so often depicted in churches in Britain seem to owe their origin to the dragons so beloved by the Celts and the early Celtic Church, rather than being based on descriptions of the more complex Biblical monsters. However,

War memorial in Crowcombe church featuring a mosaic of St George standing above a dragon representing the defeated enemy.

from the medieval period, when depictions of dragons begin to acquire four legs, the inspiration for the way dragons looked may have come from a real 'monster', the crocodile. There are obvious similarities in its reptilian scaled body, its dangerous reputation, its ability and occasional inclination to eat humans, its huge size, clawed feet, and its long tail which can lash around dangerously and do great damage. They often bask with their mouths open, a characteristic described as 'common among dragons'. It is very rare for baby dragons to be mentioned or depicted, and exactly where these creatures came from seems to have been of little interest. Somerset has two rare baby dragon carvings, one at Crowcombe church, possibly showing a live birth, while at North Cadbury church two dragons are shown hatching from eggs. A possible interpretation of a carving on misericord (No. 30) at Wells Cathedral is that it shows a sleeping baby dragon.

In the case of Norton Fitzwarren a story says that the dragon arose from the 'corruption of many bodies', an idea dating back to classical times. There are other examples of dragons appearing following a great slaughter and in such circumstances, particularly where many bodies lay unburied, disease often breaks out and spreads among the local populace. So it is possible in some cases that the 'dragon' that lays waste the area following the battle was imagery used to represent pestilence. It may be that the use of a dragon to represent illness is represented in carvings at Wells Cathedral (p. 160) and another at the church in Queen Charlton.

Dragons are often used in art to represent the Devil, sometimes shown with a second face in the abdomen like an example at East Lyng, but were also used to stand for the 'spirit of evil' and in the medieval period were also sometimes used to indicate heresy.

A dragon with a second head on its tail, the amphisbaena, was used to represent deception (two faced), humiliation or just simply badness. The scorpion was used in medieval times to indicate jealousy or treachery and what appears to be a scorpion-tailed dragon is to be found on the Norman font in the church at Isle Abbots. In some contexts a dragon was used to represent the awesome and untamable power of nature and supernatural forces, but at the same time they seem to have been used to scare away evil spirits. This is why the Vikings often used dragon heads on the prows of their ships and why dragons also appear on the towers and other parts of many Somerset churches, performing the same function. In a number of cases a dragon is to be found on each corner of a church porch protecting the main door into the building, performing a protective role, to stop evil entering the church. Such dragon symbolism was undoubtedly very familiar to people in medieval times.

Dragons were always brave and so the dragon emblem was often adopted by armies, including those of the Romans, Celts and Saxons, as well as individual knights in the medieval period and later, to be eventually formalised into their coats of arms. Dragons were also used as powerful and evocative emblems in the crests and imagery of kings and queens from the Saxon period onwards.

Dragons, particularly in the South West, can also be a memory of a local traumatic event such as a battle or raid by an enemy. Both the Britons and Saxons, and later the Anglo-Saxons and Vikings, used dragons as battle standards or in other forms, and all of these peoples at some time clashed in battles in the West Country.

Sometimes the brave act of killing the dragon by an ancestor was claimed by a local land owning family to explain, perhaps, their right to hold estates or to incorporate a dragon in their coat of arms. These are sometimes referred to as charter myths. In the case of less noble heroes, such a claim would have given the locality some prestige and made it stand out as a more notable one than other towns and villages in the district.

A guardian dragon with a stone in its mouth, on the left hand corner of the porch at St Mary the Virgin church, Isle Abbots.

Dragon stories are sometimes used to explain local features in the landscape, why an ancient burial mound exists, the story behind a dragon carving or unknown tomb in the church, or just as good tales to entertain people with. At a time when the world was still largely unexplored and reports of newly discovered animals were a common experience, people still expected to find the many strange and wondrous beasts described in the Bible and the Bestiaries and recorded in the works of the classical authors. Books, such as *The Historie of Serpents* by Edward Topsell, first published in 1608 illustrated and described dragons in some detail:

> Gillius, Pierius, and Grevinus do affirm that a Dragon is of a·black colour, the belly somewhat green, and very beautiful to behold, having a treble row of teeth in their mouths upon every jaw, and with most bright and cleer seeing eyes, which caused the Poets to faign in their writings, that these Dragons are the watchfull keepers of Treasures.
>
> They have also two dewlaps growing under their chin, and hanging down like a beard, which are of a red colour: their bodies are set all over with very sharp scales, and over their eyes stand certain flexible

A dragon illustrated in The Historie of Serpents *by Edward Topsell, 1608.*

eye lids. When they gape wide with their mouth, and thrust forth their tongue, their teeth seem very much to resemble the teeth of wilde Swine. And their necks have many times grosse thick hair growing upon them, much like unto the bristles of a wilde Boar.

Topsell, whose book included fifteen pages about dragons, also says that 'Among all the kindes of Serpentes, there is none comparable to the Dragon, or that affordeth and yeeldeth so much plentifull matter in historie for the ample discovery of the nature thereof...'

The Italian naturalist Ulisse Aldrovandus attempted to catalogue every living creature in the world. Only three volumes about birds were published before his death in 1605, but between that date and 1688 the remainder of his work was published in parts, and volume ten was *Serpentum et Draconum Historiae Libri Duo* – 'the History of Serpents and Dragons', which consisted of two volumes.

Gradually the belief in the existence of creatures such as griffins, the cockatrice, unicorns and dragons began to wane, and by the eighteenth century most naturalists agreed that dragons did not exist. However, belief in giant sea serpents and water monsters persisted right through the nineteenth century and, taking into account the fact that many people today still believe in 'Nessie' of Loch Ness in Scotland, still persists among the population today.

It was a common belief that dragons had once lived on the earth and that therefore the legends were a memory of these. This view was reinforced when fossilized bones of dinosaurs and other animals were discovered and many credited these with being the remains of dragons or giants living before the Great Flood, during which they had been drowned.

Some of Somerset's rocks are very suitable for the preservation of fossils, and remains of both *Ichthyosaurus* and *Plesiosaurus* were found at Street and Kilve in the nineteenth century and both creatures were at one time interpreted as possibly the remains of dragons (or giants) by those with little education but a lot of imagination.

It is of interest that an almost complete fossil skeleton of a 120 million year old *Ichthyosaurus* is to be found set into the floor, near the font, in a Somerset church. St Andrew's at Stogursey acquired this addition as late as 1944 so we can be fairly confident that no-one at the time believed it was the remains of a sea-dragon, but its location within the building, close to the font, is a strange echo of the images of carved medieval dragons to be seen on fonts in other Somerset churches and elsewhere in Britain.

Once dinosaurs had been recognized as 'terrible lizards' the theory was put forward that dragons were a race memory of these great creatures. This was completely discredited when dating methods proved that the dinosaurs became extinct around sixty million years before the earliest hominoids, man's direct ancestors, appeared.

Reconstruction of an Ichthyosaur *and a* Plesiosaur *from* The World Before the Deluge *by Louis Figuier, 1867.*

Dragons evolved not by means of Darwinian evolution but from the fertile imagination of man, their characteristics due not to the principle of the 'survival of the fittest', but adopted and exaggerated from the observed behaviour or abilities of real animals such as crocodiles, lizards that regenerate limbs and tails and snakes that spit venom.

2

The Characteristics of the Dragon

Most people, when dragons are mentioned, think of a large, fire-breathing monster, with the ability to breath fire being a distinguishing characteristic. In almost all the traditional British stories of dragons, of which about ninety have survived in written form, there is mention of the dragons fiery or poisonous breath. In some cases the dragon could breathe both fire and poison! Dragon characteristics, common to almost all English and Scottish dragons include their large size, (sometimes very large indeed, although some Welsh dragons seem to have been quite small!), a scaly body with a long tail, sharp teeth, and wings that usually resemble those of a bat. The ability to fly is often a feature but no tale of a dragon battle in Britain mentions the creature making use of this ability during the conflict. Some tales describe the dragon as being like a great serpent and in these cases wings are not mentioned.

Dragons were solitary creatures (although some Welsh dragons are again an exception here) inhabiting caves, hilltops, lakes and marshes. They are usually described as very aggressive, coming out unprovoked to eat livestock from the fields, consuming or destroying crops or eating human beings if they could get hold of them. In some cases they could be kept in check by the periodic offering of a human sacrifice, usually in the form of a young virgin maid, although in other parts of the country a young man may have been offered. Somerset dragon stories don't mention sacrifice, but the carving of a naked male figure being eaten by a dragon at Norton Fitzwarren church and another naked male figure being consumed by a dragon at Brent Knoll church, suggests that Somerset dragons may also have made such demands of their neighbours. A medieval carving, now damaged, on the church of St John the Baptist at Wellington, seems to show a dragon devouring two human figures at once!

British legends always concern the predation of adult dragons, very few of the stories being concerned with the problem of where they came from, how they bred or what their young were like, although they were apparently harmless when small since there are no stories of 'baby' dragons

The legs of a naked male figure hanging from the mouth of a fourteenth-century dragon carving on the tower of St Michael's church, Brent Knoll.

attacking anyone! However, one of the Somerset stories, that of the Norton Fitzwarren dragon, explains how a dragon was generated, and there is mention of baby dragons in one version of the Aller dragon story. The 'birth' of dragons has been depicted in two medieval Somerset carvings, one at St Michael's church, North Cadbury, where a carved bench end shows dragons hatching from scaled eggs and what might be a live birth is shown on a carved bench end at The Holy Ghost church, Crowcombe.

Depicted dragons are not usually identifiably male or female and any indication of sex is extremely rare. Some obviously male Somerset dragons, however, appear in this book; one is the strange example in St Bartholomew's church, East Lyng and the other is a dragon featured on a panel below the St George scene in St John the Baptist's church, Hatch Beauchamp, which shows another very unusual feature as it appears also to be defecating!

While dragons were apparently found in all sorts of habitats, they were often associated with water or wet places such as marshes, although a number of those from Somerset showed a preference for dwelling on hill tops, especially those which have ancient hill forts on them.

Generally, the most effective way to deal with a dragon was apparently to kill it, but there are a few exceptions where the hero of the story was able to drive it away, or in the case the Carhampton dragon, St Carantoc asked it to leave the area – which it did! According to a belief still prevalent today in the village of Bicknoller at the foot of the Quantock Hills, a dying dragon would try and reach the sea. This, it is said, is why there is a Green Dragon Inn (now the Dragon House Hotel) at Bilbrook, near Dragons Cross which marks the spot where, the locals claim, a dragon died while trying to reach the sea. This relates to the story of the Dragon of Shervage Wood (p. 94). A few British dragons are described as having guarded a hoard of treasure, but this is generally a tradition associated with dragons from other northern European countries, and tradition has only one doing so in Somerset, at Castle Neroche.

Topsell, in *The Historie of Serpents* (1608), mentions how useful were parts of the dragon if you could obtain them! 'The fat of Dragons is of such vertue that it driveth away venomous beasts. It is also reported, that by the tongue or gall of a Dragon boiled in Wine, men are delivered from the spirits of the night called Incubi and Succubi, or else Night-mares. But above all other parts, the use of their bloud is accounted most notable.'

A male dragon on a bench end in St John's church at Hatch Beauchamp.

Paintings, drawings and carvings from the middle of the medieval period onwards show dragons with four legs. Heraldically, a dragon has four legs but earlier dragons are shown with two. Examples of these early dragons can be found in carvings and other forms in Somerset, some having a very early origin.

The Wyvern

Before about 1400 many dragons were depicted with two legs and wings, a form which is now known heraldically as a Wyvern. The name derives from the Anglo Saxon word *wivre*, a serpent, and this is the form that many British dragons had from the time of the Saxons or even earlier. Good Somerset examples can be seen on a stained glass window in All Saints church, Alford, (p. 106) and on a mosaic in Taunton (p. 154).

The Great Worm or Flying Serpent

The terms 'worm' and 'flying fiery serpent', both occur in dragon legends from Somerset and elsewhere in the country. The dragon encountered by the woodman in Shervage Wood is described as a 'vurm' – the local dialect word for a worm or serpent. The word 'wurm' for a dragon was used by the Saxons so has a very early origin. This form of dragon usually had wings, but appeared in the form of a terrifying giant serpent, which by implication did not possess legs, but this is not always clear from the stories or descriptions. The Great Worm of Shervage Wood 'ran away' according to the local story, but exactly how is not made clear, although neither version of the story suggests it wriggled away! An early carving of a winged flying serpent can be found in St Michaels church, Flax Bourton (p. 140).

The Dragon

During the fifteenth century, illustrations and carvings began to show a four-footed reptilian creature referred to as a 'dragon', the name derived from the Greek *drakon,* giving rise to the Old Saxon *dragan,* the Anglo Saxon *draken,* and the Middle Low German, *dragen* or *dregen.* By definition these dragons always had four feet, wings and a long tail. Within these basic characteristics there are many variations; tails vary, there are different sorts of scales and shapes of head and teeth. The wings usually resemble those of a bat, but occasionally other types are found, and while green is the most common colour for a dragon, they can be depicted in other colours. Despite variations this is the most common type of dragon to be depicted over the last five hundred years and many examples of them can be seen around Somerset.

The Cockatrice

The Cockatrice, also known as a Basilisk, was one of the strangest and most dangerous creatures to appear in British mythology and to be described in medieval Bestiaries or Books of Beasts. It had the head, comb and legs of a cock and a body that merged into a serpent's or dragon's tail. It was usually quite small and lived in small caves or even an underground burrow. All other serpents fled from it as it killed its protagonists with its poisonous breath. It killed human beings simply by gazing at them and a fleeing bird could not escape being burned up and completely consumed. However, despite this formidable 'armoury', it was possible to overcome the monster. If a weasel was put down its hole the cockatrice would flee from it and the weasel would always pursue and kill it. Humans could also overcome the creature if precautions were taken. It was recommended that the dragon slayer approached holding a mirror or highly polished shield in front of him which the creature could not see behind. When the cockatrice looked at the polished surface its venomous gaze was thrown back and so it was killed, a technique recommended by Aristotle.

The bestiaries also tell us how cockatrices were born. A cock, a full seven years old, experiences a pain in its inside and becomes aware that that it is about to lay an egg. In a great state of wonder and suffering as great a pain as any beast could suffer, it seeks a warm place such as a stable or dung hill where it lays its egg in a hole. All this time its behaviour is watched by a toad or a serpent which has smelt the poison which the cock bears in its inside, and visits the hole constantly to see if the cock has yet laid its egg. When the egg is laid and the cock has left, the toad or serpent takes the egg away to a secret place and sits on it till it hatches. It cannot be hatched in any other way. So the cockatrice hatches out and is born with the head, neck and breast of a cock and the body of a serpent or dragon.

Cockatrices are several times mentioned in the Bible: Isaiah (14:29) says: 'Rejoice not thou, whole Palestina, because the rod of him that smote thee is broken: for out of the serpents root shall come forth a cockatrice, and his fruit shall be a fiery flying serpent'.

This was a commonly described creature and its method of killing was well known. It is referred to in Shakespeare's *Twelfth Night:* 'They will kill one another by the look, like cockatrices'. The best examples of cockatrices to be seen in Somerset are the fighting pair on a Norman capital in All Saints church, Lullington and an interesting variation on a bench end in St Michael's church, North Cadbury (p. XIII).

The Amphisbaena

This creature is depicted either as a winged dragon with a second head on its tail, as on a roof boss at Queen Camel church, or as a two-headed serpent-like dragon with a head at both ends, as seen on a fine Norman carving in St Micheal's church, Dinder (p. 136). This creature appears as a decorative feature on medieval manuscripts, often incorporated into ornate capital letters and decorated page borders. A serpent amphisbaena appears in a carved bench-end at East Brent church where it forms an element of entwined initials in much the way it was sometimes used in manuscripts.

The head and tail were so alike that it was popularly supposed to be able to move either forwards or backwards. This strange animal was one of a group of serpents that appear in many early medieval works on animals, both real and imaginary. From references in the Bible it is clear that a creature having a head on its tail had a sinister significance and represented all kinds of badness, humiliation and deception.

The Ouroboros

The name is derived from the Greek for *tail biter*. This creature is usually depicted as either a wyvern or serpent-type dragon that is biting its own tail. When found in a Christian context in churches or manuscripts it represents eternity or eternal life and a very fine medieval example is to be found on a misericord in Wells Cathedral where two Ouroboros are entwined together. The creature was also used symbolically by alchemists to represent *prima materia*, the first stage in an alchemical process to create the Philosopher's Stone.

Multi-Headed Dragon

A number of medieval manuscripts depict a seven-headed dragon as an illustration to the passage in the Book of the Revelation of St John (Revelations 12:3) 'And there appeared another wonder in heaven; and behold a great red dragon, having seven heads...' In Somerset, multi-headed dragons are quite rare and don't follow exactly the description given by St John. The dragon on a stained glass window in St Pancras

An Ouroboros dragon.

An 'Arachnidraco' dragon.

church, West Bagborough has seven heads but is blue rather than red (p. 163); while the stained glass window in St Andrew's church, Wiveliscombe shows a multi-headed dragon which is red but has only two heads, both of which wear a crown.

The Arachnidraco

This is a creature with the head of a dragon on an elongated neck and a body with two legs. What differentiates it from all other dragons is a scorpion-like, venomous stinging barb at the tip of its tail. The only example from Somerset is to be seen on the Norman font of St Mary the

Virgin church at Isle Abbots (p. 146), where it was probably used to represent jealously or treachery.

The Facie Humanusdraco

Noted by Brother Ranulf, a Benedictine monk some time before his death in 1364, this dragon ravished the countryside near the City of Wells until defeated by a Bishop (see p. 98). Ranulf described it as having four feet, a pair of wings, and a human face. While the sex is not specified in this case, early medieval paintings and prints of part human and part dragon creatures almost always showed the face to be that of a woman, so it is probably fair to assume that the monster of the tale had a female face too.

The Hominoida Chlorodraco

This is a very rare type of dragon, an example of which can be seen in a stained glass window in the chapel of St George in the church of St John the Baptist, Glastonbury (plate XIV). This dragon is depicted as a naked green humanoid angel with scaly skin, a pair of horns on its head and wings like those of a bat. This may be a representation of the Devil, as he is described in the Bible An early British word for a war leader was once 'Dragon'. At the time of the first Anglo Saxon translations of the Bible, the equating of and reference to a war leader as a dragon was still current. If, in the description of the battle between St Michael and his army, and the Devil and his forces, as it is given in the Book of the Revelation of St John (12:7-9), it can be accepted that the 'great dragon' was a leader of a rebel band of angels, then the Devil was himself regarded as an angel rather than a reptilian monster. The inclusion of the word 'serpent' in the account is an alternative title, like the giving of the alternative name Satan.

Thus the depiction of a humanoid dragon, particularly in this context may, although unusual, be a reasonable interpretation of the passage:

> And war broke out in heaven: Michael and his angels fought against the dragon; and the dragon and his angels fought, but they did not prevail, nor was a place found for them in heaven any longer.

> So the great dragon was cast out, that serpent of old, called the Devil and Satan, who deceives the whole world: he was cast to the earth, and his angels were cast out with him.

Sea Dragon

The most common form is that of a 'sea serpent', which is the more usual name for this type of dragon, a large, long and sinuous creature that spends most of its time at sea but some stories tell of such dragons attacking people and villages along the coast, so at least some were capable of travelling on land for short distances as, for example, in the classical Greek story of Persius and Andromeda. Many dragons are described as inhabiting marshes, so were related to sea serpents, but the rarest of this type of monster is a winged dragon with no legs and either fins or the tail of a fish and an example of such a dragon in Somerset can be seen on a carved bench end in Halse church (p. 121).

3

Somerset's Beowulf

In England's earliest written epic poems, *Beowulf*, the hero is described performing a number of heroic deeds, including a battle with a dragon which he eventually kills but at the cost of his own life. Because of its importance in English literature it has been the subject of much study and there is evidence in Somerset, Devon and Wiltshire, all parts of the former kingdom of Wessex, that the section concerning the hero's encounter with a dragon is based on a Saxon folk tale that has its origins in a time before the Saxons settled in England.

The Somerset Beowulf

A carving on the church of St Mary the Virgin, East Stoke (Stoke-sub-Hamdon) shows a figure slaying a dragon, believed by architectural historian, Nikolaus Pevsner, to be of Saxon date, making it one of the earliest such representations in the country. The carving, approximately twenty inches (52cm) wide, now forms an external arch above a narrow window on the lower part of the north face of the tower and, as is common with early church carvings, has been reused from an earlier building (plate II).

It shows a figure, wearing a knee length suit of chain mail but no helmet. Such protection was only ever worn by the Anglo Saxon aristocracy and not by 'ordinary' warriors until the eleventh century. This figure is thrusting a spear into the neck of a long-bodied dragon that has two wings and two legs towards the front of its body, and a long tongue extending from its mouth. This is very reminiscent of the dragon described in *Beowulf* as a 'coiled, scaly creature which could fly'. Between the dragon slayer and the head of the monster is a sword.

The identity of this dragon slayer is not known, but because of its early date (sometime between the seventh and tenth centuries) a number of dragon slayers can be ruled out. Of the three Somerset saint's associated with dragons, St Carantoc, St Dubricius and St Petroc, none were described as having killed or attacked their dragons - they used their 'faith' to deter them.

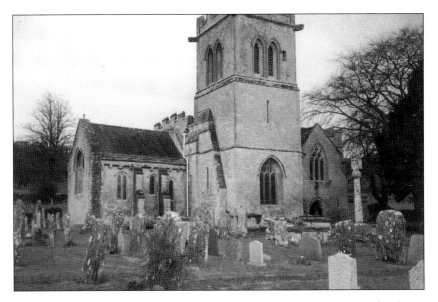

St Mary the Virgin church, East Stoke, has probably the earliest carving of a dragon slaying to be found in Britain.

The East Stoke figure is not St Michael, who is always depicted with wings, and as the carving is in such good condition, it can be seen quite clearly that this figure does not have them; nor can it be St George as his fame did not spread in England until the crusades from the twelfth century onwards. So who is this very early Somerset dragon slayer? The answer lies in the poem *Beowulf*.

The Poem

Beowulf is a poem of 3,183 lines, preserved, almost complete, in a tenth-century manuscript now in the British Library in London. It is generally regarded by scholars as the most important of the nation's epic works to have survived, as well as being the earliest and most complete piece of English literature. It is believed to have been written between AD 700 and AD 1000. It concerns the Danish King Scyld Scefing who, quite early on in the poem, dies and is placed on a boat laden with arms and treasures and sent out to sea. Next is mentioned his son and grandson, Beow and Healfdene but these are quickly passed over and the next person encountered is Hrothgar, the son of Healfdene, who builds a splendid hall in which to entertain his retinue. However, the hall is attacked at night by a terrible monster called Grendel, who kills up to thirty warriors at a time. No one can withstand him and, despite sacrifices, the hall remains empty for twelve years. At the end of this time, Beowulf, a nephew of Hygelac, King of the Geatas, and a man of enormous strength, decides to go to the aid of Hrothgar. He embarks with fourteen companions and sails for Denmark where he eventually defeats both the monster Grendel, and Grendel's mother who lives in a pool shadowed by trees but apparently connected to the sea.

Much of the poem is taken up with anecdotal tales concerning various characters and adventures, as well as a lot of genealogical information. In the poem a long time is supposed to have elapsed, Hygelac has fallen and his son, Heardred, was slain by the Swedes, and so Beowulf becomes King of the Geatas. He reins gloriously for fifty years until his kingdom is attacked by a dragon. This encounter is described in an account on page 36.

The Characters in the Poem

Scholars have identified real incidents and people mentioned in the poem to arrive at a date for the original poem, of which the surviving manuscript is a copy of an earlier work, which itself is most likely to be copied from an earlier work that was probably derived from several earlier, possibly oral, sources.

Some of the events and earlier adventures of Beowulf in the poem are closely matched by other stories such as an incident in the Scandinavian *Grettis Saga* where the hero Grettir, kills two demons, one a male the other female. This story is set in Iceland, but so close are some details in the two stories that they must share a common link. The hero of this story is Grettir, who appears to have been a real person who died about 1031, and it's probable that an earlier traditional Scandinavian folk tale has become attached to his name. The same story was also credited to a Prince of the Geatas, the Gauter people of old Norse literature, represented today by the people of Gotaland in the south of Sweden.

So it would appear that *Beowulf*, in the form that it has survived, is actually made up of different folk tales from various parts of Scandinavia and north Germany, although it is generally agreed that the surviving manuscript was written in England by someone who created this impressive poem by drawing on a variety of earlier sources. It must have thrilled those who heard it recited by storytellers as they sat round a flickering fire in their ancient halls.

The Saxon's first came to England in AD 449, initially as mercenaries to aid the Britons but later they turned on their employers and so began a wave of invasion and settlement. They came from north Germany and various parts of Scandinavia. The Saxon's who were to eventually settle in Somerset came from the area of Germany known today as Lower Saxony, and described by the historian Bede in 731 as 'Old Saxony'.

The *Anglo Saxon Chronicle* records the events:

495. There came two ealdormen to Britain: Cerdic and Cynric his son, with five ships to the place called Cerdicesora.

508. Cerdic and Cynric killed a British king named Natanlaod, and five thousand men with him.

514. The West Saxons came into Britain with three ships to the place called Cerdicesora.

519. Cerdic and Cynric received the West Saxon kingdom, and the same year they fought with the Britons, in the place now called Cerdiceford; the royal line of Wessex ruled from that day.

These Saxon's, under their leader Cerdic, who became the first King of Wessex, first settled in the Surrey and Hampshire area, but because of resistance by Briton's to the west had to fight their way westwards under successive Kings and did not settle in Somerset until the seventh century.

The Wessex Connection

Examination of the poem's linguistic and metrical characteristics lead us to believe that it was originally composed in a northern or midland's English dialect, the area occupied by the Mercians who had come to England from an area that is today part of the province of Schleswig-Holstein, at the neck of the Danish peninsula. However, the surviving manuscript in the British Library is in the West Saxon form of English – that is, the dialect spoken by the people of the Kingdom of Wessex. In its present form the poem dates from Christian times as it contains a number of passages of a Christian character, but there are also many pagan references which come from the earlier version, such as the ship burial of King Scyld Scefing, and indeed the hero of the story, Beowulf himself, is eventually given a non-Christian funeral ceremony and is buried with a great treasure under a huge burial mound. It seems not to be a Christian work with pagan undertones, but a pagan work that has been given a Christian revision in later versions.

Four separate elements or lays for the incidents in the poem have been identified, one of these, the section dealing with Beowulf's fight with the dragon, is stylistically quite distinct from the rest of the work and almost certainly a separate story which has been incorporated into the main poem.

Who was Beowulf?

As the existing manuscript is in Wessex English, it is possible that a Wessex bias has been given to the story too. In the poem the hero's name is given as Beowulf, but a similar name occurs among the supposed ancestors of King Cerdic, although these are generally regarded as being 'mythological'. This is Beaw, a shortened form of Beowulf, who was the son of Scyld Scefing, both of whom are mentioned in the poem. The description of the dragon incident, because of its exciting nature would, one might expect, have made a great impression on most audiences who heard this long and complex poem with the next most memorable encounter, perhaps, being the fight with the monster Grendel and his mother.

It is probable that the dragon story existed in its own right in both Saxony and later in Wessex, before it was incorporated into the longer poem. The dragon story may also have been credited to Beow, one of King Cerdic's ancestors, as although Beow and Beowulf are treated as separate persons in the existing poem, and indeed from separate countries, the whole area of north Germany and Scandinavia shared much in common in the way of folk tales and legends, and many aspects of these seem to have been interchangeable.

It was also not unusual for Royal families to claim decent from heroes and gods, so for King Cerdic to have a heroic, dragon slaying ancestor would have been very prestigious and something his successors and the Saxon people would almost have expected. Dragon slaying stories elsewhere have been recorded relating to more than one person: St George, for example, is credited with the dragon slaying deeds of Persius. This dragon story also quite clearly has its origins in northern Europe, as Scandinavian/Germanic dragons have specific characteristics. The author of *Beowulf* does not identify his fearsome dragon with the Devil, despite the fact that he was obviously a Christian, but Scandinavian dragons almost always seek out treasure and their main role in life is as treasure guardians. This behaviour is rare in ancient dragon legends from Britain and other parts of the world.

As the Beowulf story has its origins in northern Europe the story obviously came to England with the Saxons so must pre-date their arrival. The fact that Beowulf's adventures were known in Wessex is further supported by the occurrence in ancient charters of the now obsolete local names *Beowanham* and *Grendles Mere* in Wiltshire and

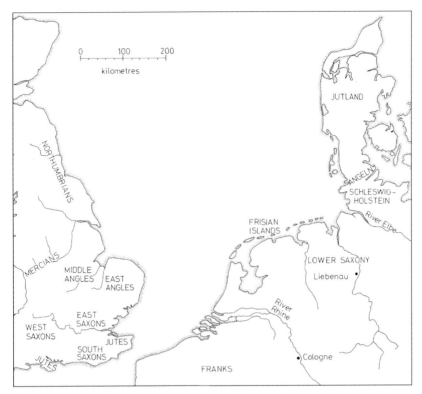

The West Saxons, who were to populate the Kingdom of Wessex came from the area of northern Germany now known as Lower Saxony.

Grendeles Pytt in Devon. This is probably a local attribution of Beowulf's encounter with the monster Grendle to a location in England, much as St George was credited locally with killing his dragon in the Vale of the White Horse in Oxfordshire. So the carving on East Hamdon church most likely illustrates the brave deed of Beowulf, or Beow, in killing the dragon, and while it does not show exactly the way the dragon was fought and killed as described in the *Beowulf* manuscript, this may not be too unexpected if it illustrates a 'local', and perhaps simpler, Wessex version of the story. It appears in the church, presumably, to illustrate how the hero overcame adversity and got his reward, even though this was in heaven.

The carving is of enormous importance therefore as being possibly the earliest English example of a dragon slayer at work, and illustration of a dragon legend whose origins lie so far back in time that its beginnings are in the homelands of the Saxons in the fourth century, or almost certainly even earlier.

35

With the coming of the Norman's in the eleventh century, the Germanic and Scandinavian connections were broken, and the story of Beowulf was forgotten until its rediscovery by historians in the nineteenth century.

The Story of Beowulf and the Dragon

After many adventures and brave deeds, Beowulf became King of the people known as the Geatas. He ruled wisely for fifty years until one day a dragon appeared. This dragon lived in a stone roofed burial chamber under a large earth burial mound where it guarded a great hoard of treasure, put there by an ancient people now long gone. There was a hidden passage into the burial chamber and one day a slave, who had run away from his master, found his way down this passage to where the treasure was hidden and discovered the guardian dragon asleep. This slave had fled the heavy hand of his master, but when he realised where he was he panicked, grabbed an item from the treasure and fled from the place.

The dragon had guarded this treasure for three hundred years, and while the people of the country were in fear of it they had had no trouble until this day. The slave stole a golden cup and took it to his master asking to be reinstated into the household. This request was granted but when the dragon awoke it saw that someone had entered its dwelling place and stolen part of its treasure and its fury was aroused. It rippled down the rock, writhing in anger. The dragon circled round and round the burial mound, scorching the ground in its anger, searching for the person who had disturbed its slumber and stolen from its hoard, but no man was to be found.

It waited impatiently for nightfall when it would punish those who caused it to be disturbed and dared to steal its golden cup. Eventually night fell, and the dragon burst forth from its lair, spewing out great flames, and the houses of the people were burnt, and the glow of the burning buildings could be seen for miles around. The dragon ravaged the Kingdom, flying from place to place and leaving a trail of havoc and destruction in its path. As dawn approached, it returned once again to its lair. Behind it the land was swathed in flame, with fires burning everywhere, and night after night the destruction was repeated. News of the dragon was brought to Beowulf and he learned that his people had suffered greatly, and that even his own house, the most splendid of buildings, the throne room of the King, had been burnt and was nothing more than ashes. Beowulf was anguished and fell into a dark mood. He knew in his heart that he had no choice but to destroy the dragon. He ordered a shield made of iron from his blacksmith, as the King's wooden shield would not have withstood the fiery breath of the dragon. Beowulf was too proud a warrior to fight the dragon with an army and would face the foe alone. He had been in dangerous situations before and he did not fear the creature despite its strength and courage.

Beowulf gathered together a small band of warriors, eleven in number, along with he who had stolen the golden cup and thus brought trouble on the people. He was forced to join them as their guide since he was the only person who knew the location of the underground passage in the burial mound. The burial mound was sited on a headland by the billowing sea. In this burial chamber, full of treasure, the dangerous dragon stood guard over its remaining hoard.

Beowulf sat on the cliff top and spoke to the warriors who accompanied him. He first wished them luck as he felt a sadness in his heart - a feeling that death might be near. He then told them how, as a young man, he had often risked his life, but that now he was an old man and as the King and protector of his people, he had no choice but to pursue the fight. He told them that he would prefer not to use a weapon to defeat this evil if there was any other way, but he would be meeting molten venom in the fiery breath of the dragon, so he would go forth in a shirt of mail and with his specially wrought iron shield. He ordered his warriors to remain where they were, safe in their armour, as it was his duty alone to pit strength against the monster. He would either win the gold by his courage or die in mortal combat.

Beowulf stood up in his war shirt and helmet and went to confront the dragon. He came to a stone arch by a gushing stream that issued from the burial mound, boiling with a deadly heat as it flowed from the dragon's resting place deep inside. He knew it would be hard to overcome the heat of the dragon's lair so he gave a great shout to draw out the creature, expressing his anger at the destruction in his Kingdom. His voice resounded around the rock and penetrated to where the dragon waited. It recognised a human voice and burst forth, fired up for battle. Beowulf raised his sword and the dragon turned on the King, who stood, his sword raised ready in his hand. Both combatants were aroused to a great fury, both striking terror in the other.

The King held his shield before him and the dragon writhed and breathed out flames before racing at his challenger. His shield saved him from the first onrush and he raised his hand and struck hard at the shining scales of the dragon. The first blow cut the dragon's hide and it writhed on feeling the blow and spewed more flames. As the combatants clashed again the guardian of the treasure gained confidence and Beowulf was wreathed in flames and feared the worst. No help was at hand as his warriors were afraid and had fled on seeing the dragon - all except one man. His name was Wiglaf, son of Weohstan, who remembered how Beowulf, had given him gifts and welcomed him into his household. He could not stand by or flee so with his wooden shield in one hand and his sword in the other went to fight beside his lord, his first in such a desperate battle. The two stood together and the dragon attacked again. The young warriors armour was near useless against such a foe but his shield, though charred gave some protection after Beowulf's shield had shattered into sparks and ashes. With Wiglaf at his side, the King took heart, now inspired by thoughts of glory, the King swung his sword with all his strength at the head of the dragon but his trusty weapon shattered. Then the dragon attacked again, seizing its chance, and lunged at Beowulf, clamping its fangs around the King's neck whose body now ran with blood.

Wiglaf, seeing the King's peril, changed his attack from the dragon's head to its belly and, although his fighting hand was burned, thrust in his sword and the fierceness of the fire from the dragon's mouth was lessened. The King gathered his strength and drawing a sharp knife, kept on his belt, stuck it deeply into the flank of the dragon delivering a fatal wound. The dragon was defeated. The wounds inflicted on the courageous King began to scald him and a poison began to spread through his body. He knew his wounds were mortal but in spite of them Beowulf spoke to Wiglaf saying 'Go quickly, bring out the treasure so that I may see it and my going will be easier for having gazed upon it'.

Wiglaf went into the mound and there he beheld a great and sight - there were wall hangings and gold spread across the ground, golden goblets and vessels, arm bands and helmets - a great hoard of treasure. Soon after this the King died. The treasure had been won but it was paid for with his life.

The people built a great pyre for their King, placed helmets and war shields on it and laid his body in the middle. They kindled the largest of all funeral pyres and then built a great earthen mound over the site filling it with the treasure from the dragon's hoard in honour of the King.

4

The Dragon Slayers

Not all heroes who fought and disposed of dragons were knights in shining armour, armed with swords and mounted on white horses. In fact, legends concerning dragons describe a very wide range of heroes. Occasionally it was an anonymous knight, such as the one who engaged a Somerset dragon at Churchstanton. More often the knight is named as a local landowner, or becomes a landowner once he has defeated the dragon, and his descendants proudly maintained the story of them acquiring their land or titles due to the bravery of their ancestor. In medieval times many saints were followed who are now almost forgotten, some of these were involved with dragons. Somerset's representatives in this respect include St Carantoc and St Dubricius, who both lived in the sixth century.

However, in many cases these dragon slaying heroes were of a more lowly status and followed such occupations as farmer, woodcutter, blacksmith, farm labourer or simply a 'brave man of the village' - with no specific occupation mentioned. In most stories these heroes of humble stock had no material reward beyond the grateful thanks of their neighbours.

Somerset's dragon slayers include Saints, a bishop, a knight a landowner, a woodman and villagers working together; a number of them do not have their occupations or names described.

In most instances, knights use the expected weapons of their class, the sword and spear; while dragon slayers of a lower class use tools such as axes, scythes, or their natural cunning to defeat the dragon by trickery. An exception might be the story of John Aller who killed the Aller dragon. He is usually described as being of humble origin, but according to the story, he used a spear, the weapon of a knight, although in an alternative version he is described as a lord. So the spear would be a more appropriate thing to use, and as a Sir John Aller did actually exist, this would indicate the story describing him as a knight or lord is the more correct one, although the origins of the story probably go back a couple of centuries earlier. Multiple versions of a story co-existing in one area are not uncommon and are also seen elsewhere in Britain.

5

Dragon Saints

Many saints encountered dragons, forty of them in the western church alone, some only locally famous. These legends usually describe religious procedures used to overcome the dragons rather than combative ones.

Tales of saints that meet dragons are usually allegorical stories demonstrating the holiness or goodness of the saint in overcoming Satan, or used to symbolise the victory of the saint (Christianity) over the pagans. Common elements in the stories include banishment, driving away with Holy water or binding with a priestly stole (scarf) rather than killing.

Many of these legends date back to the early Christian era when missionaries were going out to convert the Saxons, Danes, Norsemen and others to the 'true' religion.

Somerset saw the arrival of missionaries from an early date, and according to legend, even some of Christ's disciples visited Glastonbury in Somerset and helped build the first church in Britain. On firmer ground, many of the Somerset churches do have an early Saxon origin when the religious ceremonies and beliefs of the South West followed those of the Celtic rather that the Roman church. It therefore follows that many of these churches were dedicated to Celtic saints whose names are now little known. Following the Norman invasion in the eleventh century, many of these churches were rebuilt or enlarged and it was probably at this time that they were rededicated to more mainstream saints. In such a dragon conscious county, as is clear by the surviving evidence that has come down to modern times, it was perhaps not unnatural for the superstitious medieval mind to be drawn to 'dragon orientated' saints, and feel that dedicating their church to such a person would be a good omen for the district.

The medieval clergy, although more educated than their congregations, still saw the world as being inhabited by various forms of evil spirits that could cause mankind problems. This was reinforced by the

Bible, where many such evil manifestations took the form of dragons. So they too, might have been inclined towards the adoption of a dragon defeating saint, especially in areas where stories of these creatures were still prevalent among the country folk.

The images of the 'dragon saints' in Somerset appear in a number of forms ranging from medieval carvings on bench ends to stained glass windows. While a First World War memorial in Crowcombe church, features an impressive little mosaic of a victorious St George standing above a defeated dragon representing the vanquished enemy, an image used on a number of war memorials in the county in which, sometimes, St George is also accompanied by St Michael.

Some saint images lost for centuries or destroyed during the turmoil of the civil war and the Cromwellian period in the mid-seventeenth century, when so much church carving was lost, have been replaced in recent years. Notably an interesting representation of St George over the porch at St George's, Bicknoller and a St Michael in the niche on the tower of St Michael's, Enmore. This was replaced in 1979 to mark one hundred years service by the then Rector, Robert Jones and his father who was Vicar at Shepton Mallet for forty-nine years. What makes this of particular interest is that Robert Jones was the model for the St Michael statue!

The grouping of churches dedicated to 'dragon saints' seems in one case to be of some significance. Clustered near the edge of Carhampton marsh where St Carantoc defeated a dragon according to a legend going back to at least the tenth century, can be found in close proximity to churches dedicated to St Carontoc (at Carhampton till demolished around the four-teenth or fifteenth century), St Dubricius (Porlock), St George (Dunster), St Michael (Minehead) and St Petroc (Timberscombe). All are of an ancient foundation, and to have so many churches dedicated to dragon associated saints in the vicinity of a well known dragon site, is unlikely to be just a coincidence.

While St George was well known and popular throughout Britain from the thirteenth century, the people of Somerset claimed a very personal connection with him as they believed he had actually visited Glastonbury. Of the four hundred and eighty one Somerset churches dedicated before 1800, fifty-eight of these are dedicated to saints who have a dragon 'connection'. There are forty churches dedicated to St Michael: Angesleigh, Bawdrip, Blackford, Brent Knoll, Bath St Michael, Brushford, Burnett, Butcombe, Chaffcombe, Clapton in Gordano, East Cocker, Compton Martin, Creech St Michael, Cudworth, Dinder, Enmore, Flax Bourton, Greinton, Haselbury Plucknett, Henstridge, Ilchester, Milverton, Minehead, Monkton

Combe, North Cadbury, Orchard Portman, Othery, Penselwood, Puriton, Raddington, Rowberrow, Runnington, Seavington St Michael, St Michaelchurch, Shepton Beauchamp, Somerton, Stawley, Stoke St Michael, Twerton and Weyford. St George claims eleven: Beckington, Bicknoller, Dunster, Easton-in-Gordano, Edington, Hinton St George, Rushton, Sandford Brett, Wembdon, Whatley and Wilton. There are five dedicated to St Margaret: Babington, Middle Chinnock, Queen's Charlton, Thorn St Margaret and Tintinhull. There are churches dedicated to St Petroc and St Dubricius at Timberscombe and Porlock, respectively and, there was once a church to St Carantoc at Carhampton.

St Carantoc

A Celtic saint who is patron saint of Carhampton in Somerset where he had an encounter with a dragon and was patron of Crantock in Cornwall and Llangranog in Wales also. He built a monastery in Somerset, and was the leader of a group of monks who evangelised Somerset and central Cornwall in the sixth century. He went from there to Brittany, where he was known as Caredoc. The full story of his adventure with a dragon in the Carhampton marshes is described on page 77.

St Dubricius

He was a Welsh bishop, also known as St Dyfig, and is believed to have died in about 550. Little is known of his history, but he was one of the earliest and most important of the saints of South Wales who worked also in the Hereford area as well as bringing Christianity to the South West. He seems to have landed in Porlock on the Somerset coast as a missionary, and according to a local tradition lived there till he died at the age of one hundred and fifty years. The historian Geoffrey of Monmouth claimed, somewhat improbably, that he crowned King Arthur, and later officiated at the marriage of King Arthur to Guinevere.

The Tale of St Dubricius and the Dragon Scaring Bell

Dubricius, a holy man lived at Porlock and built a wayside chapel, St Saviours, between Horner and Luccombe at the foot of a terrible mountain track across the great hill called Dunkery Beacon. When the bell of this chapel was rung its sound rang out across the moorland and all the dragons and other hideous fiends that dwelled there were

The remains of St Saviours chapel, built by Dubricius in the sixth century, in which was hung a bell to scare off dragons.

compelled to withdraw deeper into the moor so keeping the way safe for the passage of travellers. Under the alter of the chapel St Dubricius buried a chest full of gold, to be spent on keeping the bell in order and giving charity to all who dared to cross the dreaded waste alone to earn their market monies. The site of the ruined chapel can still be seen today beside the coach road, but nobody has found the gold!

For many centuries people believed bells could ward off harm and possessed magical powers. They often bore an inscription such as *Voce mea viva depello cuncta nociva* (With my voice I get rid of harmful things). It was believed that bells spoke with the voice of God and the power of the bells reached as far as they could be heard. The word bell is derived from the Anglo Saxon *bellan*, which means to bellow.

St Petroc

The most famous of the Cornish saints, he was said to be the son of a Welsh chieftain who, after studying in Ireland, made his way to Cornwall and founded monasteries at Padstow (Petrockstowe) and later at Little Petherick where he also built a mill and a chapel. He later lived as a hermit on Bodmin moor and, like other hermit saints, is said to have had a special affinity with animals, relevant to one of his two dragon encounters! He is sometimes depicted with a stag in memory of the animal he sheltered in his cell from huntsmen on one occasion. On his death he was buried at Padstow which became the centre for his cult. His relics were stolen from the abbey at Bodmin in 1177 and ended up in a French abbey from which they were retrieved following the intervention of Henry II. Many churches were dedicated to him in Cornwall, eighteen in Devon and one in Somerset.

The Tale of St Petroc and the Fearsome Dragon

In those days, Tandurus reigned in that part of Western Britain. He was a man of fierce and cruel ways who, in his savage tyranny, had gathered together worms and all sorts of poisonous serpents into a great pit of water used to punish and torture thieves who were thrown into the pit. After Tandurus had died the son who succeeded him forbade the use of such tortures. Soon the famished serpents rose to the surface of the water in the pit in a writhing mass and gnashed at one another with their vicious fangs, so that soon, out of their great number, there remained but one alive. This was a horrible monster with a great body that left the pit to tear apart any cattle and men it could catch in its huge jaws. Then one day there came to this place Petroc, a man of God, who saw that this great serpent had killed a man. He thereupon knelt on his knees in front of the gathered people and prayed that life be restored to the man. His prayer was granted and the man lived. Petroc then ordered the fearsome monster to depart to a wilderness beyond the seas and never to harm anyone again. This the huge serpent did and was never seen again.

St Petroc and the Injured Dragon

There was a certain large dragon that used to come wondering around the cell of Petroc, a Holy man of God and this dragon got a piece of wood lodged in its right eye, and sensing that this good man could help it, the dragon expelled harmlessly all its venom and hurried to the place where the Saint was praying. There it patiently stood for three days, waiting for the saint's favour. At last he took pity on the poor distressed creature, and by order of the blessed Petroc the dragon was then drenched with a liquid which was sprinkled over it, mixed with the dust from the paving stones. Such was the strength of this medicine and the power of the saint that it at once drew the piece of wood from out of the dragon's eye, whereupon it went back healed to its solitary lair.

A More Recent St Petroc Story

After tracing the dragon to its lair the saint finds the dragon asleep:

> His mouth half-open, snoring loud and fierce,
> A leg part-eaten thrusting out between
> His awful fangs; his black and stinking tongue
> Lolls about, and quivers, covered up with flies
> And all about the bones and offal lie:
> Rejected stench of former prey of his.
>
> So still and calm he stands, does Petroc now,
> Signing the cross before the creature's gaze –
> Breathing a psalm into its horrid ears –
> Now see! The dragon eyes him quietly,
> And even sits to lick his outstretched hand.
>
> So Petroc led the docile creature down
> To the sandy seashore, where amid the waves
> The last great Cornish dragon swam away,
> Bound for what strand or desert island far
> We none of us can tell.

St George

The best known of dragon slayers is St George. He is believed to have been a Roman soldier who, as a Christian, publicly tore up an edict of the Emperor Diocletian (285-313) against the Christian churches in Nicomedia, (modern Izmit in Turkey). His arrest and execution can be precisely dated to AD 303. He was buried at Lydda in Palestine and his martyrdom was recognised quite early as is shown by a Greek inscription, dated 346, found in an ancient church at Ezra in Syria.

The tomb of St George was encountered by knights on the first crusade to the Holy Land in 1099. His image appealed to them as he was also a warrior saint who had given his life for Christ just as they were prepared to do. It was not long before they began to invoke his name as a battle cry. At the Battle of Acre in 1104, St George himself is said to have appeared among them and the crusaders won a decisive victory. This confirmed the 'power' of St George and the knights adopted him as their unofficial patron saint.

His appeal was very great and on the return of the knights from the crusades St George's popularity became very widespread. During the third crusade, 1189-92, King Richard I invoked St George as the patron saint of his army and in 1222 he displaced St Edward the Confessor as England's patron saint. The date of 23 April, the supposed date of his execution, was designated as his feast day.

The cry 'Saint George!' was also used at the Battle of Poitiers in 1356, at Shrewsbury in 1403 and both the cry and the banner of St George were used at the Battle of Agincourt in 1415 and Bosworth in 1485.

St George's fame and appeal spread throughout England and local legends grew up about him, including the claim that he had visited Somerset! (See p. 47)

So, where does the dragon come in? It so happens that a few miles from St George's tomb at Lydda is Joppa, the legendary site of a battle between the Greek hero Perseus and a great sea dragon that had come to take away the maiden Andromeda.

The crusaders probably heard stories about this battle between a hero and a dragon, and as it was supposed to have taken place so close to where St George's tomb lay, the tale became associated with him. It is interesting to compare the story of Perseus's adventures, which were related by Ovid in his work *Metamorphoses*, with the classic tale of St George and his encounter with a monster.

The story of St George and the dragon first appears in print in the *Legends Aurea* by Jacques de Voragine which was written in the thirteenth century. This was unquestioned by both the church and laymen in the medieval period. The dragon was mentioned in the office books of the church, and priests using the Sarum Missal sang on St George's day a song in Latin, that included the line 'Royal maiden saved from the fearful dragon'. This persisted until Pope Clement VII removed the reference from the missals and breviaries in the Reformation following Henry VIII's split with the papacy.

The Tale of Perseus and the Sea Dragon

Cassiopeia, Queen of the Ethiopians, was so proud of herself that she dared to compare her beauty to that of the sea nymphs, which so angered them that they sent a great sea dragon to ravage the coast. To appease the sea nymphs Cassiopia's husband, King Cepheus, was told by an oracle to sacrifice his only daughter Andromeda to be devoured by the monster. Perseus saw the virgin chained to a rock awaiting the dragon. He went to her and asked her name and why she was bound to that spot. Andromeda explained about her mothers pride and that the only way to satisfy the sea nymphs was for her to die. Just then a great noise was heard and the sea dragon appeared, its head raised as it swam towards the shore. Andromeda screamed, and her parents, who had now arrived on the scene, began to cry. Perseus said to the king and queen that he would fight the dragon and if he won he wanted their daughter's hand in marriage. To this they at once agreed. Perseus then jumped onto the back of the dragon, avoiding its fangs, and thrust his sword between its shoulders, this enraged the creature who turned out to sea, and Perseus, clinging to its back, plunged his sword between the monsters scales until eventually it died.

The Tale of St George and the Dragon (according to Jacques de Voragine)

George, a Roman tribune, was born in Cappadocia, and came to Lybia and the town called Silene, near which was a pond infested by a monster. This creature had many times driven away armed hosts that had come to destroy him. It had even approached the walls of the city and, with his exhalations, poisoned all who were near. To avoid such visits, it was supplied with two sheep each day, to satisfy his voracity. If these were not given he attacked the walls of the town so that his poisoned breath infected the air and many of the inhabitants died. He was supplied with sheep until these were exhausted and it was impossible to procure the necessary number. Then the citizens held counsel and it was decided that each day a man and a beast should be offered, so that at last they gave up their children, sons and daughters, and none were spared.

The lot fell one day on the princess. The monarch, horror-struck, offered in exchange for her his gold, his silver and half his realm, only desiring to save his daughter from this frightful death. But the people insisted on the sacrifice of the maiden and all the poor father could obtain was a delay of eight days in which to bewail the fate of the damsel. At the expiration of this time the people returned to the palace and said 'Why do you sacrifice your subjects for your daughter? We are all dying before the breath of this monster!' The king felt that he must resolve on parting with his child. He covered her with royal clothes, embraced her and said: 'Alas! dear daughter, I thought to have seen myself re-born in your offspring. I hoped to have invited princes to your wedding, to have adorned you with royal garments, and accompanied you with flutes, tambourines and all kinds of music; but you are to be devoured by this monster! Why did I not die before you?' Then she fell at her father's feet and sought his blessing. He gave it to her, weeping and clasping her tenderly in his arms. Then she went to the lake.

George, who passed that way, saw her weeping and asked the cause of her tears. She replied, 'Good youth, quickly mount your horse and fly, lest you perish with me!' But George said to her: 'Do not fear. Tell me what you await and why all this multitude look on.' She answered: 'I see that you have a pure and noble heart, yet fly !'

'I shall not go without knowing the cause,' he replied. Then she explained all to him. Whereupon he exclaimed: 'Fear nothing. In the name of Jesus Christ I will assist you.' 'Brave knight,' she said, 'do not seek to die with me. Enough that I should perish, for you can neither assist nor deliver me, and you will only die with me.'

At this moment the monster rose above the surface of the water. And the virgin said, all trembling, 'Fly, fly, sir knight!' His only answer was the sign of the cross. Then he advanced to meet the monster, recommending himself to God. He brandished his lance with such force that he trans-fixed the dragon and cast it to the ground. Then he bade the princess pass her girdle around it and fear nothing. When this was done the monster followed like a docile hound. When they brought it to the town the people fled before it. But George called them back, bidding them put aside all fear, for the Lord had sent him to deliver them from the dragon.

Then the king and all his people, twenty thousand men without counting the women and children, were baptised, and George smote off the head of the monster.

Saint George – The Somerset Connection

In medieval times the battle between St George and the dragon was claimed by some to have taken place at one of two sites in England; Brinsop in Hertfordshire or at Dragon Hill, just below the Uffington White Horse chalk figure in Oxfordshire. Somerset was not to be left out! There was never a claim that St George had fought his dragon in the county but it was said that the great dragon slayer had visited the holy site of Glastonbury. On St George's day a procession and festival was held for many centuries and there was an alms distribution to the poor. There was a chapel of St George in the now ruined Glastonbury Abbey, which was restored in 1418 and a new alter was consecrated and a painted banner of St George placed in it. Even more interestingly, there was a 'relic' of St George kept there under lock and key. There was also a large carved image of St George in the abbey and it is recorded that in 1500 the horse required a new tail and that John Chyverton regilded the image, which must have been a great deal of work because he was paid the sum of £6 13s. 4d for it.

There is still a chapel dedicated to the Saint in the local church of St John the Baptist, along with other St George items of interest (see page 141). Further St George references can be found in the town. The beautiful pilgrims inn, built by Abbot Selwood at the end of the fifteenth century, now called The George and Pilgrim's Hotel, used to feature a sign of St George killing the dragon. It still features St George on its sign today, (plate IV) but now he is shown holding his newly acquired sword aloft, with a group of monks and nuns in the background, but it no longer shows a dragon.

The stone shields on the front of the inn are of particular interest because they confirm that local belief in the St George connection was current in 1475 when the inn was built. The arms of England, surmounted by the rising sun of the House of York are in the centre, to the left is the shield of St George, a red cross on a white background, and to the right is a blank shield. The latter is a feature in the local legend of St George.

The Legend of St George - How his sword was won at Glastonbury

It was said that George was born at Coventry, the son of a nobleman called Albert, and that his mother died in giving birth to him. In the grief and mourning that followed he was abducted from the castle by an enchantress called Kalyb, and he grew up in her charge. When he came of age she gave him a horse called Bayard, a suit of armour and a shield that bore no device or coat of arms as Kalyb did not wish him to learn whose child he was. She gave him no sword as she told him he would find one for himself. One day George, in company with six knights he had delivered from Kalyb's spell, arrived at Glastonbury. Here it was said, could be found the Holy Thorn that grew from the staff of Joseph of Arimathia and the Holy Grail. The abbey also housed the sword, called 'Meribah', claimed to be the one with which St Peter struck off the ear of Malchus, servant of the High Priest, in the Garden of Gethsemine. This sword Joseph was also supposed to have brought with him to Britain.

When the seven knights arrived, the blank shield of George excited attention as normally all shields bore some identifying emblem and when the Abbot was told of it he invited the knights to the abbey and entertained them. After supper, the Abbot told them about the sword 'Meribah', and how a wicked knight had sworn to get hold of it. The Abbot was very afraid that he might succeed in seizing it, but the knights vowed they would not let this occur and George was chosen to meet the wicked knight in battle. As he did not have a sword, the Abbot lent him 'Meribah'.

Arms on the George and Pilgrim Hotel at Glastonbury. Built by Abbot Selwood in the fifteenth century it shows the two shields of St George, one of which is blank in keeping with local legend.

They rode at each other full tilt with their lances seven times, the other knights looking on. At the seventh encounter, both were unhorsed and George was wounded under the left shoulder, blood gushing down his blank shield and then when he fell, across the shield sideways. As George rose to his feet to continue the fight the knights saw the blood red cross of Christ on his white shield, which from then onwards was the emblem that he always bore on it.

George drew 'Miribah' and the two knights swung their swords at each other, but George's sword shattered that of the other knight as the two weapons clashed. The wicked knight was now at the mercy of George but he spared his life and bid him ride away. The Abbot then presented the sword to George, who carried it from that time on in all his wonderings in Palestine and Egypt and used it in his famous battle with the dragon.

St Margaret

It is likely that St Margaret is not a historical figure but a character in pious fiction. In one version of her story it is said she was a victim of the Diocletian persecutions so putting the date of her supposed martyrdom

St Margaret escaping from within the dragon on a bench end carving in St Michael's church, North Cadbury.

in the early fourth century. Her name first appeared in the western church in the ninth century but she became famous in the time of the crusades in the eleventh and twelfth centuries. Veneration of St Margaret became very popular in England in the later Middle Ages particularly because of promises she made at the end of her life.

According to the Sarum Breviary she promised that 'those who write or read her 'history' will receive an unfading crown in heaven, that those who invoke her on their death beds will enjoy divine protection and escape from the devils, that those who dedicate churches or burn lights in her honour will obtain anything useful they pray for, and that pregnant women who invoke her will escape from the dangers of childbirth, as will their infants'. The latter relates to her adventure with a dragon.

The Tale of St Margaret and the Dragon

Margaret, was said to have been the daughter of a pagan priest, Sedisius of Antioch, but she became a Christian against her father's wishes. He turned her out of the house and she was forced to live as a shepherdess. Olybrius, governor of Antioch, carried her off to his palace to either seduce or marry her. She proclaimed herself to be a Christian and refused his advances. Olybrius, furious at this rejection, had her tortured and thrown into prison. While awaiting execution she prayed to see her real enemy, the Devil, who had brought all these events about. Her prayer was granted and a huge and frightful dragon appeared before her.

There are various versions of what happened next. Some say she gathered herself together, despite her fear, and held out her crucifix in front of her, whereupon the dragon vanished. Others claimed she was actually swallowed by the monster, but then either cut her way out of the belly of the creature using her crucifix, or made the sign of the cross inside its stomach, whereupon the dragon burst asunder and she stepped out unharmed.

St Michael

Michael was an archangel, whose name means 'Who is like unto God'. In the Book of the Revelation of St John he is the main fighter in the heavenly battle against the Devil who is depicted as a dragon. In the *Testament of Abraham* Michael is the principal character whose intercession is so powerful that he can even rescue souls from hell and in some representations he is shown with a pair of scales weighing up the souls to assess their worthiness for being saved.

The cult of St Michael began in the East, where he was invoked for the care of the sick. His fame and popularity spread to the west from the

A stained-glass window at Michael's church, Milverton showing St Michael fighting a dragon. The artist's inspiration may have come from the modern monitor lizard, the so-called Komodo Dragon.

fifth century onwards and his cult was strong in Britain from early times, with many churches dedicated to him. Many high places are also associated with him and bear his name. In art he is commonly represented as slaying a dragon. His battle with Satan in the form of a dragon is graphically described in the Book of the Revelation of St John:

> And war broke out in heaven: Michael and his angels fought against the dragon; and the dragon and his angels fought, but they did not prevail, nor was a place found for them in heaven any longer.

> So the great dragon was cast out, that serpent of old, called the Devil and Satan, who deceives the whole world: he was cast to the earth, and his angels were cast out with him.

6

Dragons in Heraldry

Heraldry has its origins in the crusades which began in the eleventh century. As the armour worn by knights became more elaborate it enclosed their bodies and hid their faces so making them difficult to recognise in battle. To overcome this each knight decorated his shield with some easily recognised and characteristic pattern. These designs or symbols were often based on a real or imaginary animal. So it was that shield decoration became formalised as heraldry. Heraldic shield designs were inherited and so became part of the identity of a family.

A tunic, the surcoat, was worn over the armour, and this too was embroidered with the knights chosen emblems and it was this garment, the 'coat of arms', that lent its name to the elaborate shields and emblems that developed in later centuries and are still used today.

To further help identify an individual, particularly from the early thirteenth century when the closed helmet was introduced, knights placed prominent ornaments on their helmets. This could take many forms such as eagles, feathers, a dagger and a large variety of other easily identified things and this became known as the crest. A number of knights wore a dragon crest of various designs and colours.

By the beginning of the fifteenth century these symbols and emblems had become so important that they were carefully 'guarded' by the families that had developed them, and a College of Heralds was set up to regulate who could use them, ensure symbols were kept distinct for each user and to design new ones for people who did not already have them or for families who had coats of arms but had become united by marriage.

The dragon, as a symbol for strength, bravery and national unity was used by members of the Royal family. Thus King Richard the Lionheart carried a lion standard in the 1191 crusade and Henry III used it in a campaign against the Welsh in 1245, but it did not form part of the Royal armorial bearings until Henry VII took the red dragon of Cadwallader as part of his arms to acknowledge his Welsh ancestry. He claimed uninterrupted decent from the British kings Uther and Arthur, and his emblem

A dragon crest on the seal of Roger de Quencey, Earl of Winchester who died in 1264.

was Y Ddraig Coch – 'red dragon' of Wales. A contemporary writer described this as 'A dragon grete and grymme, full of fyre and eke venymme'. Henry VII used the dragon as a supporter to the shield bearing his arms, with a white greyhound on the other side.

The use of a dragon emblem by the supposed King Uther is given in the *Flores Historiarum* :

> Uther Pendragon, father of Arthur, had a vision of a flaming dragon in the sky, which his seers interpreted as meaning that he should come to the kingdom. When this happened, after the death of his brother Aurelius, he ordered two golden dragons to be fashioned, like those he had seen in the circle of the star, one of which he dedicated to the Cathedral of Winchester, and the other he kept by him to be carried into battle.

A dragon was used by Henry VIII as a supporter, and later by Elizabeth I, who changed the colour of the dragon from red to gold, but James I had it replaced by the Scottish unicorn. It saw a brief revival as a supporter in the Arms of Oliver Cromwell, Lord Protector of England in the Commonwealth period (1649-60), but it did not survive the Restoration of Charles II.

The seal of the Earl of Lancaster, showing he used a dragon crest on both his helmet and horse. His coat of arms also has dragon supporters.

According to Dennys in *The Heraldic Imagination*, about two hundred English families feature a dragon on their coat of arms, and about three hundred European ones. Heraldic dragons can be found used in the crests of some Somerset families, for example the Fitzwarrens, the Herberts at Kingston St Mary and the Somervilles at Dinder, the latter two have church monuments on which wyvern dragons can be seen. Dragons on coats of arms can also be seen on public buildings around the county, particularly in Taunton, the county town, and even on lamp-posts in the more architecturally sensitive areas.

The Heraldic Dragon

The head of the dragon is like no other 'animal' found in heraldry, and whether designs of the early heralds were pure imagination or influenced by the head of the crocodile is not known. The heraldic dragon has a neck covered in scales, like those of a fish, as also are its back and legs, each of which ends in clawed feet. The underside has ring scales that extend down the legs.

The tongue is usually barbed and the main heraldic variation in dragons is found in the shape of the ears, but the wings are always like those of a bat, with long bones or ribs that extend to the edge and base of the wing.

In nearly all modern representations of dragons in heraldry the tail ends in a barb, although most dragons of the medieval period are represented with a long, smooth tail ending in a blunt point. Heraldic dragons

Dragon rampant.

Dragon passant.

Dragon stantant.

are usually shown in one of three positions: *passant* - with one leg raised, *stantant* - with all four legs on the ground and *rampant* - rearing up with one leg on the ground. The latter is the attitude of the Wessex dragon used by the county of Somerset (see cover). Other positions, such as crouching, are known but these are very rare.

The Heraldic Wyvern

The wyvern has exactly the same head as a dragon, but in English heraldry its body differs considerably. It has only two legs and a body that narrows into a looped tail that terminates in a barb. Its body has scales on the back and ring scales on the breast and underside of the lower body and tail.

The wyvern is usually shown resting upon its legs and tail but occasionally it is shown sitting upright on its tail with its legs in the air. There are rare examples showing a wyvern without wings.

Wyvern.

Wyvern with wings displayed.

Wyvern erect.

Cockatrice.

The Heraldic Cockatrice

The cockatrice, also known as a basilisk, is comparatively rare in heraldry, the main difference between a wyvern and a cockatrice is that the dragon's head is replaced by that of a cock, whose beak, comb and wattles are usually shown in a different colour to the rest of the body. The neck may either have scales or feathers that blend into the scaled body.

The Heraldic Hydra

This is usually shown as a seven-headed dragon as described in Greek mythology. It is very rare in heraldry and is used as a crest by only three English families.

The Heraldic Amphisbaena

This is the rarest of all heraldic dragons, is double-headed and vomits fire at both ends. It is used as a crest by one English family, the Maules.

7

The County Arms of Somerset

Today the arms of the county of Somerset show a red dragon rampant, holding in its forelegs an upright blue mace, all on a gold background. However, the counties of England were latecomers to the idea of adopting heraldic arms to represent them. Somerset County Council came into being in 1889, but there appears to have been no thought given to an official coat of arms for some time after that. The county justices used a seal for their official notices that showed King Ina of Wessex sitting in judgment, but this was not thought to be an appropriate emblem for a purely administrative body, so the Clerk of the Council was asked at the second council meeting to obtain a design for a seal. A seal was accordingly designed and authorized and consisted of a dragon rampant surrounded by a wreath bearing the words 'Administrative County of Somerset'.

Since the council had no formal coat of arms some councillors, interested in heraldry, looked into the matter and, as Somerset had formed part of the old Kingdom of Wessex, felt that the county was entitled to display the arms of that Kingdom. Fortunately for Somerset, none of the other Wessex counties had adopted the dragon, so it was open for Somerset to do so. These unofficial arms, which were not registered at the College of Heralds, bore a golden Wessex dragon on a red background and were adopted by the council in 1906. In 1911 an offer to officially register the arms was made by William Bucknell Broadmead of Enmore Castle, High Sheriff of the County. Mr Broadmead also paid the cost of registering the arms, which were given official recognition on 2 December 1911, when Somerset County Council was granted its coat of arms by the College of Heralds. However, the arms were altered slightly from the unofficial ones used up to then, making the dragon red on a gold background, described heraldically as *Or, a dragon rampant gules* and giving it a mace to hold. The council ordered a new seal to be made, 'at a cost of no more than twenty pounds', and this came into use from 26 November 1912.

Somerset's present coat of arms outside County Hall, Taunton.

As we have seen, dragons have long been associated with Somerset. It was said that a great dragon fought on the side of King Cerdic, the supposed founder of the West Saxon Kingdom about AD 519, (of which Somerset was a part), and helped him to repulse an attack by his enemies. According to a medieval chronicler, Henry of Huntingdon, writing in the twelfth century, the West Saxons had used it as their emblem from the middle of the eighth century, and the later West Saxon kings bore the image of a dragon on their battle standards. Certainly, when King Cuthred met the Mercians in battle at Burford in 752 he was fighting under a dragon standard. The army of Wessex was led by Alderman Edelhun 'who bore the King's ensign in a golden dragon'.

A similar standard is mentioned as being used by Edmund Ironside in his battle against the Danes in 1016 and dragon emblems which

The unofficial coat of arms used by Somerset County Council between 1906 and 1912 on the former Somerset College of Art, Taunton.

Section of the Bayeux Tapestry showing two Saxon battle standards with dragons, one of which has fallen.

were cut out and fixed to a staff, are clearly shown being carried by the Saxons on the Bayeux tapestry, made about 1077, which depicts the Battle of Hastings in 1066.

The arms of the West Saxons were shown on the title page of of a set of maps by John Speed, published in 1610, under the title *Theatre of the Empire of Great Britain*, on which he shows a gold dragon on a red background, a colour scheme that inspired the unofficial county arms, but which was to be reversed for the official arms of Somerset. The motto that appears below the shield, *Sumorsaete Ealle*, means 'All those of Somerset', and was taken from a passage in the *Anglo Saxon Chronicle* which refers to events that took place in 878:

At Easter, King Alfred, with a little company, built a fort at Athelney, and from the fort kept fighting the force [Danes], with the help of those of Somerset who were nearest. In the seventh week after Easter he rode to Ecgbryht's Stone, east of Selwood. *All those of Somerset* came to meet him, and those of Wiltshire, and Hampshire, the part of this side of the sea; they were glad of his coming.

They finally pushed back the Danes so ending the threat of a Danish occupation of Wessex.

8

Dragon Stories

Somerset, like many other counties, has tales of local dragons but more of these tales seem to have persisted into modern times than in other places and so the county, particularly the western side, has a lot of dragon 'evidence' in one form or another.

The legends were passed down through the generations largely as oral tradition. In the telling parts would have got left out, especially when they where no longer fully understood, while other bits would be added. In some cases the heroes name may have got changed. Sometimes legendary or historical characters sharing the same name become confused between stories confounding modern attempts to trace the origins of folk tales.

Parts of other dragon tales may have been introduced as the storytellers encountered them and adding other embellishments to increase the excitement and amazement of the audience must also have been a temptation from time to time. Most of the legends only came to be written down in the late nineteenth and early twentieth centuries. An exception is one concerning Bishop Jocelyn's encounter with a dragon near Wells that was recorded before 1364 and another is the Carhampton Dragon tale that was published in 1516.

When early records of folk tales were made the recorders did not always note full details of a story, as they were related by the teller, only a summary was made. Some of the stories that appear below are short and give only the gist of a tale and we may assume that it was just these details, perhaps with local significance, that would have kept the audience of original listeners enthralled in their halls, cottages or inns, lit by candle or lamplight.

Considering the dwelling places described for dragons in both Somerset and elsewhere, it seems few were associated with places that were commonly regarded as being haunted, sinister or 'evil' such as graveyards, ruins, the location of gallows and gibbets, or cross roads, all places regarded with superstitious dread in the past. They also do not seem to be generally associated with prehistoric monuments with the exception of hillforts, a favourite dwelling place for Somerset dragons, so while representing evil as far as the church was concerned, dragons to the common people represented a dangerous, but not necessarily evil monster, but something resembling the wild beasts, like those they had heard about in far away places like Africa.

Nor do dragons seem to have been regarded as part of the supernatural world inhabited by ghosts, spirits, goblins, the 'little ones', demons and other such creatures, belief in which persisted in parts of the West Country until quite recent times. Indeed, the appearance of so many dragon carvings on the outside of church buildings seems to have been to deter 'attacks' on the building by evil spirits.

Dragons in Somerset do not seem to have been regarded as living in the far distant past, but were considered to have been around in quite recent times, not perhaps when grandfather had been alive, but quite possibly in the time of his great grandfather!

Dragon beliefs in Somerset are reinforced by the geography of the county, particularly of the western side where most of the stories and 'evidence' are to be found. Until recently it was an area of low population, thick mysterious woodlands, extensive misty marshes and a wild, largely deserted coastline - just the sort of places where dragons might have lurked.

The industrial revolution had little effect on Somerset, and did not lead to huge numbers of people deserting the countryside for the cities, so families remained in the same locality for generations, and it is this settled pattern that enabled the dragon legends to come down to us today.

Although people regard dragon legends as being based on the imagination of the storytellers, as an historian once said, 'tradition is generally an accretion of error formed upon a nucleus of truth, and there is a danger, if we cast away the tradition too hastily, that we may cast away the truth with it!'

In some cases there are indicators within a story that suggest it is of very ancient origin and some parts of it may have some basis in fact - the 'dragon' being a folk memory, passed down the generations for a thousand or more years, of real incidents that affected the district in some traumatic way. Examples of this are the Norton Fitzwarren Dragon story (p. 86) and the Aller Dragon story (p. 72).

In Celtic Britain the word 'dragon' came to be used for a chief or warlord. In Welsh *draig* is the word for 'dragon', but it can also mean 'chieftain', 'leader', 'warrior' or 'military power'. There are many examples from Welsh Celtic literature where the war leader is referred to as a dragon. A leader was referred to as a 'Pendragon' when leading a band of warriors from different tribes or groups in times of trouble, and tradition says that the father of the famous King Arthur was Uther Pendragon.

When such a leader was killed in battle, the warrior who had carried out the deed was said to have 'slain a dragon'. In a poem by the Bard Taliesin about the hero Gwallaec, he tells how the warriors lamented the death of their 'dragon'. It may be this use of the term for a leader of a band of warriors that explains the origins of some of the dragon legends that are of undoubted antiquity.

Visualise a man in, say the thirteenth or fourteenth century telling his son how his father told him that his great-great-grandfather was a very brave man who had fought and killed a dragon — but this term for an early leader having been forgotten, the incident was now visualised as a fight between his ancestor and a fire breathing monster. This version of the story, with exact details becoming more and more unclear as time passed, persisted into recent times, sometimes with the name of the hero being lost or the deed attributed to someone else — so no matter how unlikely the tale sounds it may well contain a grain of truth.

The Viking Connection

Like many areas of Britain Somerset suffered many traumatic Viking raids in the ninth century. The *Anglo-Saxon Chronicle* is a good indicator of the frequency and size of these incursions that were violently resisted by the West Saxons with varying degrees of success. The first recorded raid was in the year 836: 'King Ecgbryht fought with twenty five ship companies at Carhampton and there was great slaughter; the Danes held the battlefield'.

Attacks came in various parts of Wessex and there was another in 843 when 'King Aethelwulf fought at Carhampton against the companies of thirty-five ships, and the Danes had the power of the battlefield.' Two years later, in 845, 'Ealdorman Eanulf, with the men of Somerset, Bishop Ealhstan and Ealdorman Osric, with the men of Dorset, fought at the mouth of the Parret with a Danish army and there made great slaughter, and took the victory.'

The attacks and invasions were taking place in many parts of the country, and by 870 the Viking's had taken all England except Wessex, and the following year King Alfred of Wessex made 'peace' with them, which lasted until 876 when Wessex was again attacked.

After a number of reversals of fortune, Alfred finally won a decisive victory at Edington in Wiltshire and the leader of the raiders was converted to Christianity at Aller in Somerset. However, Viking raids were to continue at intervals over the next one hundred and fifty years; Exeter was destroyed, for the second time, by a Danish force in 1003.

As some of the Viking ships bore the head of a dragon on the prow it is easy to see how these terrible attacks could have become associated over a period of time with dragon legends. The Viking ships had a very shallow draught enabling them to penetrate up rivers and into the marshes so prevalent at that time in Somerset, so it is easy to imagine what terror must have been struck in the hearts of villagers as they spotted these 'dragons' coming out of the marshes with the threat of devastation that was to follow. Many of the dragon stories of Somerset are found in areas that suffered Viking raids, so it is possible that some of these stories arise from tales of raids and battles between the people of Somerset and the Vikings in the ninth and tenth century.

Somerset has an interesting example of a dragon story that not only dates back to the fourteenth century and is well remembered in the district, but is commemorated in a traditional play that constantly evolves and changes. This is to be found in the area near the City of Wells where a play about the slaying of the Worminster dragon is performed every fifty years – to prevent the monster re-appearing. Because of the long intervals between performances it is re-written each time it is presented, so it not only keeps the tradition alive, but ensures its survival because it can be adapted to be topical and of interest to each generation that sees it.

Place name evidence is found in many parts of Britain where a partic-ular hill, standing stone or burial mound has a dragon related name incor-porating such words as 'worm', 'dragon' or 'drake' (a local term for dragon in some parts of Britain). Early examples are Drakelow in Derbyshire, mentioned in 772 (when it was Draca Hlowe), and the Drake or Dragon Stone mentioned in 1651 at Stinchcombe, Gloucestershire. In many cases there is a tale attached to the feature that explains its name in terms of connection to a dragon that has hidden its treasure there, been killed at the spot, or is buried there, and so on. Somerset also has some examples: there is 'Dragon Cross' near Old Cleeve, which is near the former Green Dragon Inn (now called The Dragon House Hotel). This is a small cross road with a tall war memorial near it in the form of a stone cross that has a large bronze sword on it, and is said locally to be the spot where one half of the dragon from Shervage Wood is supposed to have died; and it is also said to have been visited by the Minehead Sailor's Horse during its annual outings at one time.

Near the village of Thurloxton there is a Green Dragon Hill, often described by people travelling over the hill, along the Taunton to Bridgwater Road, as a lonely and eerie spot where rocks on both sides of the road stood up prominently. It was apparently a particularly fright-ening place after dark, especially for children riding home on their bikes. The road has now been remade since the beginning of the twentieth

A war memorial by a small cross roads at Bilbrook, known locally as 'Dragon Cross', is said to be the spot where the dragon from Shervage Wood died.

century when such recollections were last heard. The origin of the name has now been forgotten, but it is unusual in that a colour was assigned to the dragon. There are other dragon or worm hills in various parts of Britain, but colours are rarely mentioned. If it was once associated with a local dragon legend, as seems likely, this has not come down to us.

Brent Knoll, north west of Burnham on Sea, is a steep-sided, conical hill that has an Iron Age hillfort on its summit. Locally a smaller flat-topped hill to one side of this is called Dragon Hill. Many of the Somerset dragons were described as living in these ancient hill forts and there is believed to have been a legend about a dragon associated with this one but details are now lost.

Local tradition also claims that a great battle was fought under Brent Knoll 'once upon a time'. Could this have been the battle recorded in the *Anglo Saxon Chronicle* for 845, when the men of Somerset and Dorset banded together and defeated a group of Danes? If so it may be the origin of a dragon story and the place name.

It is also interesting to note that the ancient parish church is

The Dragon House
Hotel, Bilbrook.
Formerly the Green
Dragon Inn, it is situated
near Dragon's Cross.

dedicated to a dragon slayer, St Michael, and even more significantly, a Hunky Punk carving on the church shows a naked man being devoured by a dragon, perhaps illustrating an aspect of this legend and indicating its ancient origin?

A field on a farm at Churchstanton is called Wormstall, and said to be the place where a dragon was killed. Worminster Sleight lies just south east of the city of Wells, and locally is believed to have been associated with the dragon that devastated the surrounding countryside until slain by Bishop Jocelyn in the thirteenth century (see p. 96). Unfortunately, authorities on the origin of place names disagree: Robinson says it is derived from the Old English *wor, mynster* and *slaed* which means 'the moor church valley'; while Hill suggests it is a vagrant form of *Waermunder Slaed*. The term *Waermunder* comes from Old English meaning 'True Guardians'. This valley gave access to the Court Barons held at Dinder, and the *Waermunder* was a Saxon order of Knights who saw their role as upholding the common law.

The Dragon of Aller

Aller is a small village on the marshy Somerset Levels and offers two or three versions of a dragon story. It is an example of a legend that describes its hero as either, a local working man, John Aller, or as a landowner or a knight. Records confirm the existence of a Sir John Aller, who died around 1272. His family owned the manor of Aller from at least 1166, but this individual is the only one referred to as Sir John Aller or John of Aller.

In Aller church is an effigy of a knight, now defaced, that is probably Sir John, and local legend has it that this is indeed the tomb of the dragon slayer. There are clues within the dragon story to indicate that it is of considerable age. One is the claim that John Aller 'plastered his body with pitch'. The tale gives no explanation for this, but it is known that if a medieval warrior could not afford chain mail, he would soak his clothes in pitch, then roll in sand which stuck to the pitch and formed a protective coating. There is an example of this described in one of the Icelandic Sagas, where the hero, Ragnar Lodbrok, did this before he fought a dragon.

Another indicator that the story is an ancient one is that the dragon is described as a 'flying serpent', the term used for dragons in the early medieval period, the four legged creature that most people visualise as a

Dragon Hill, the local name of a hillock on the side of Brent Knoll which can be seen here on the right.

dragon appears somewhat later. Early dragon stories also tend to describe the monster as having poisonous breath, rather than spewing forth flames.

The Aller story has elements in both the versions that are found in dragon legends from other parts of Britain such as the liking of dragons for milk, which in some cases led to their downfall; the fact that in one version the dragon slayer is himself killed shortly after destroying the dragon; and that the dragon's blood caused all the plants to die where it was spilt, and they had not grown properly there since.

These fascinating tales also include some rare aspects, such as the mention of baby dragons; and the fact that the actual weapon that Sir John is supposed to have used to kill the dragon is still in existence. This spear was originally kept in the belfry of Aller church, but is now kept at Low Ham church. It has an iron spear head 45 cm in length, mounted on a shaft 2.44 m. in length that seems to have been made of four lengths of light wood with what appears to be a leather covering. The shaft is painted in bands of brown, green, red and yellow with rings of black in between, with wide variations in the width of the various bands down its length.

This story is well established locally and so it is worth considering its possible origins. It may be a tale originated by the holders of the manor of Aller to justify their ownership of the estate; or to prove to the peasants how the family was the 'protector' of the area. The Aller family may also have 'modified' a dragon legend that already existed in the area. A similar origin for the Norton Fitzwarren dragon has also been suggested (see p. 87). If this is the case, then the origins may lie further back in history, again like the dragon story from Norton Fitzwarren. Aller is in an area that was subject to raids by Vikings in the ninth and tenth centuries. Raids took place in Somerton, only five miles from Aller, in 877, Norsemen were active in the Bristol Channel in 893, and there was a battle at Watchet on the Somerset coast in 918 when a large party of raiders were driven off 'with great slaughter'. Perhaps this dragon legend is based on the stories of local people who, under the leadership of a local man, repulsed a raid by the 'dragon men' on one of these occasions? Over the centuries details would be forgotten and the story may then have evolved into this dragon tale.

A poem was published by Mrs Spillsbury in 1894 which she called 'The Legend of the Dragon of Aller Hill'. She also thought the dragon represented marauding warriors, but in her case she attributed the origin to Saxon raids, but this did give her the opportunity to mention King Arthur.

The tomb of the reputed dragon slayer, John Aller, in St Andrew's church, Aller.

The Legend of the Dragon of Aller Hill

From Arthur's tent the 'Dragon' waves on high,
Lit with the splendour of the sunset sky,
Sign of the great Pendragonship, the crest
Which Cerdic from the King would gladly wrest;
Cerdic the Saxon! who, with haughty will,
Plants the same standard upon Aller Hill,
Making incursions on the country round,
And ravaging each hide of conquered ground.

And Cerdic upon Aller Hill abode,
Still harassing with many a fierce inroad,
The humble dwellers of the peaceful vale;
Till, as the years flew by, arose the tale,
When Arthur, "Flower of All the West", was
gone,
And Britain's darker days were drawing on,
The people, groaning, 'neath the Saxon sway,
Spoke of "the Dragon" that, from day to day,
Flew forth from Aller, with his fiery breath,
Striking the poor and weak with instant death.
The monster swept their flocks and herds away,
Bore off the children at their harmless play.

The spear that local legend says was
used by John Aller to kill a dragon.

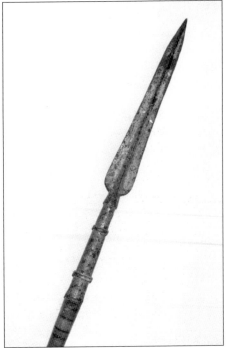

The iron spear head of the weapon
said to have been used by John Aller.

The Tale of the Dragon of Aller

This poison-breathing monster, which had the shape of a great flying serpent and was protected by an armour of scales, lived in a den on the south side of Round Hill above the village of Aller. It descended to devastate the villages in the marshy valley, and wherever it flew the crops and trees were poisoned.

Milkmaids fled at the first hiss of its wing-beat; and a score of pails had their contents drunk in a few minutes, much to the consternation of the girls who milked the cows each day. People lived in dread of a horrible death for themselves, their children, and their cattle.

At last a knight called John of Aller, or the Lord of Aller, came boldly to their rescue. He plastered his body with pitch and put on a mask so that the dragon's breath could not harm him; and he armed himself with a long spear specially fashioned for this exploit. He journeyed to the dragon's den, and attacked it while it slept. After a fierce fight in the darkness, he killed it. Seeing two or three baby dragons in the den, he went home to fetch several of his labourers to stop up the hole with the spikes of an iron harrow. After that day nothing would grow near the hollow place in the hill except elder trees.

The Dragon of Aller – a second version

Many years ago a fiery, flying dragon lived at Curry. It flew from hill to hill over the marshes leaving poison wherever it landed, and at certain times it used to fly across the marsh to Aller and destroy the crops and all it came near with its fiery breath.

At last one John Aller, a brave and valiant man who lived at Aller, vowed that he would kill it. He lay in wait, and when next the dragon flew across to Aller Hill he attacked it, and after a fierce struggle slew it and cut off its head.

Then its fiery blood ran out and scorched up all the grass around and from that day to this grass has never grown on that spot. John Aller was so burned by the dragon's breath that he died almost at the same moment as the dragon. The people took up his body, buried it in the church, and called the village after him. If you go into the church you can still see today the tomb of John Aller, the brave dragon slayer who sacrificed his life to save his fellow villagers.

This story was first recorded in 1885,and the local farmer who related it to a folklore 'collector' pointed out a bare patch on a hill as the site where the dragon was killed.

The Carhampton Dragon

This dragon lived in the Carhampton marshes, now drained, to the east of Minehead. It was quelled by an early saint of the Celtic church, Carantoc, who is believed to have lived in the sixth century. It is said he had a miraculous stone altar which he set afloat on the Severn Estuary so it would guide him to the spot where God wanted him to build a church. The stronghold of King Catho mentioned in the tale is identified as Dunster Castle, the dragons lair as Ker Moor and the land granted to Carantoc as Carhampton. This version of the story was printed in medieval Latin by Wynkyn de Worde in 1516.

The Tale of the Carhampton Dragon

In those days two Kings, Arthur and Catho, reigned over that region, and Arthur had come there to find a certain huge and terrible serpent which had devastated many fields. Carantoc came and greeted Arthur, who gladly accepted a blessing from him, and the Saint asked him if he had heard whereabouts his altar had come to shore. The King said, 'If my request were granted, I would tell you.' 'What request do you want to make?' asked the Saint. The King said, 'That you should remove the serpent which is near here, if, as it seems, you are a servant of God.' Then Carantoc prayed to the Lord; and the serpent came to him straight away with a great roar, like a calf running to its mother, and bowed its head before the servant of God like a slave obedient to his master, humble and gentle-eyed. The Saint then placed his stole round its neck and led it away like a lamb. Its neck was like a bull's neck, and the stole would hardly go round it. In this way they went to the stronghold and greeted King Catho, who received them kindly. Carantoc led the serpent into the middle of the courtyard and some people tried to kill it, but the saint would not allow it to be killed. The Saint then led it out of the gate of the stronghold and released it, ordering it to depart and never to dare harm anyone again.

As a result of this, Carantoc not only got back his wonderful altar, but was given the stretch of land beside a river mouth where it had come to land and was allowed to build a church there.

A second version of the Carhampton Dragon story exists. This version, later than the previous one, has a lot more detail and is almost as if the storyteller had been there at the time! A chapel of St Carantoc stood on the site of his oratory for several centuries, serving as the parish church as late as the reign of Edward II (1307-27). The likely site of this chapel, below which stood St Carantoc's oratory, is the garden or orchard adjoining the former vicarage at Carhampton which stands three hundred yards (91m) to the east of the present church. In 1994 excavations revealed the cemetery that was probably associated with the church of St Carantoc. The church of St John the Baptist has three very fine and large dragons on the tower which was completely rebuilt in 1870.

The Tale of the Carhampton Dragon: a second version

When King Arthur was a young man he ruled the country around Dunster jointly with a chieftain called Cadwy. There was a great dragon which ravaged the countryside round Dunster and the adjacent villages of Carhampton, then called Carrum, and Old Cleeve. The inhabitants petitioned Arthur and asked him to rid them of this great monster. At that time the region consisted of a huge marsh between the sea in the Severn Estuary and the densely wooded land. Arthur set out to hunt the dragon, following its tracks for miles over the marsh and down to the sea shore where he saw it swimming far out at sea.

The local inhabitants had told him that even the most fearless hunters were helpless against this dragon which destroyed their crops, devoured their animals and even the shepherds and herdsmen, and carried off any children it could catch.

Dunster Castle, built on the site of Catho's stronghold, where St Carantoc led the dragon he had subdued.

One of three large dragon gargoyles on the tower of St John the Baptist church, Carhampton, looking out over the marshes where St Carantoc had his encounter with a dragon.

As the King watched the dragon swimming in the waves, its great body undulating among the waves, he noticed a strange stone object floating towards him.

When the tide cast it up on the beach, he saw that this piece of stone was banded with beautiful colours and to his amazement recognized it as an altar. He picked it up and decided to keep this miraculous item for his own use.

The next day it came to his notice that a strange man, wearing a sheepskin and carrying an ash staff, was wandering around asking the peasants if they had seen an altar washed up by the sea. This little man had made several journeys down to the shore and returned carrying large stones that he piled up in a solid place on the marsh, saying he meant to build an oratory and set his altar in it. His name was Carantoc, and it was said that he was the heir to the Welsh kingdom of Ceredigion, but as he had been called by God to renounce all earthly riches, so he had left his father's court, put on the clothing of a shepherd and crossed the Severn. As he approached the English coast he threw his portable altar out of the boat so that God should reveal the place where he must set it up. He landed on the outskirts of the Carhampton marsh and sat down under a tree waiting for a divine sign to direct his actions. As he meditated, he started to make a staff from a rod of ash he had cut in the woodland, whittling away the rougher part with his knife so that the shavings fell upon the ground. A wood pigeon flew down and carried off a wood-chip in its beak. Carantoc watched the pigeon fly away and followed it across the marsh convinced this was the sign he had been waiting for. Eventually the pigeon dropped the wood-chip on the ground and when Carantoc found it he knew that God was telling him this was the spot where he had to build his oratory. In later years this was replaced by the Chapel of St Carantoc.

King Arthur encountered the holy man near the shore and when Carantoc asked Arthur if he had seen an altar cast up by the sea, he replied that he would give it up if the saint would help him. Carantoc asked what he required and Arthur pointed to the huge coiling dragon swimming in the sea. He told him that Carrum had been devastated and the people killed, and said: 'If you are the Lord's servant rid the people of this monster and your altar shall be restored to you.' Carantoc then knelt to pray on the shore before wading into the sea and calling to the dragon across the water. Whereupon, the monster swam obediently towards him and uttered a gentle, welcoming cry.

When it came close, the saint threw his scarf about the great scaly neck, which was so thick that he could only encircle it with difficulty and the dragon 'used no wing nor claw' but let the saint lead him, docile as a lamb, across the marshes into Cadwy's stronghold on the height now occupied by Dunster Castle.

The dragon stood, quiet and friendly, on the rush-strewn floor of the Great Hall. At first the warriors wanted to kill it, but Carantoc forbad this. Soon the people forgot their terror and crowded round him. The saint then commanded the dragon to do no more harm and sent it out through the gates, and it went to live peaceably in some lonely place on the marsh far away from the dwellings of man. Arthur then handed the altar back to Carantoc, who carried it away and placed it in his stone oratory.

The Dragon of Castle Neroche

On a spur of the Blackdown Hills near Broadway, close to Illminster, is the impressive earthworks of Castle Neroche, a Norman motte and bailey castle probably built in 1068. This was constructed on an earlier fortification that was later abandoned. Its name is probably derived from Nerechich - a place where hunting dogs are kept, as the Neroche Forest was one of five royal forests in Somerset.

There are a number of legends associated with the earthworks suggesting that a great treasure is hidden there protected by the Devil.

The Tale of the Dragon of Castle Neroche

There was a dragon that lived in a deep hole in the ancient hill fort called Castle Neroche. It used to come out, particularly at night and attack travellers on the road below the hill fort, kill them and take their treasure back to its lair. Everyone knew it was there, but were too afraid to venture near it or attempt to kill it. This went on year after year, and steadily its hoard of treasure grew.

However, one day a local man plucked up the courage to approach the dragon's lair. He peeped inside and saw the dragon sitting on its great hoard of treasure. He quietly crept away and gave a lot of thought to the problem of tackling the dragon. He sat by a spring that was gushing forth water that ran away in a stream. All of a sudden he had an idea. He ran back to his village and explained his plan.

The next day the villagers quietly returned with him to the spring and dug a new channel in the hillside that took the water from the spring to the lair of the dragon where it poured into its hole and drowned the monster.

Later, when the water had soaked away, the villagers entered the dead dragon's lair and collected its great hoard of treasure and everyone became rich.

The Churchstanton Dragon

Churchstanton lies nine miles (14.4 km)south west of Taunton. There is no village centre as such and the buildings are scattered. The church, dedicated to St Peter and St Paul, is possibly on the site of a Celtic or Saxon church, or where a hermit's cell once stood. Its name is derived from the Saxon 'Estanton' – Stony Town. The present name of Churchstanton dates from about 1555. There is a dragon carving on a bench end in the church dating from the fifteenth century, but it is not prominent and is therefore not likely to have been responsible for the local dragon story, nor does it illustrate it. There are no other dragon carvings on this simple and attractive church which appears to have escaped the attentions of Victorian restorers.

It is interesting that a second local legend says that the hill where the dragon story is sited was also once the site of a battle but no details remain of this, and the people who told of the two legends do not connect the two, regarding them as separate events. However, is it possible that this dragon story, like others, may be a tale of a Saxon or Danish battle with local people and the details have become split into two stories and the details of which had almost been completely lost when finally recorded in the early twentieth century? A more recent version of the story claims that the hero in the story was one of King Arthur's knights.

The Tale of the Churchstanton Dragon

In this region, long ago, there lived a dragon that caused the inhabitants of the district a lot of trouble and levied a great toll on human life. They lived in fear of this monster, until one day a valiant knight, whose name has now been forgotten, came to the area and engaged the dragon in combat. After a fierce fight, the knight finally overcame and killed the creature. As it died the dragon thrashed around with its huge tail and furrowed up the ground in the field where it died, and these marks of its dying can still be seen to this day to remind everyone of this knight's brave deed.

An early name for a dragon was a 'werme' and this field, part of Stapley Farm, is called Wormstall – the place where the dragon was stopped.

Kilve's Drowned Dragon!

Chance findings of the fossilized bones of dinosaurs or other large extinct creatures such as mammoths may have, from time to time, given rise to dragon stories although there is no direct evidence of this ever happening in Britain. However, in Europe there are several examples where such finds were displayed as the remains of dragons and in China most fossil bones were credited to dragons until quite recently.

The fossil skull of an Icthysaurous, a large water dwelling dinosaur, was found at Street in the late nineteenth century and a subsequent tale arose that this was the remains of the dragon of Kilve which follows here but presumably this was devised as a 'good story' rather than a real belief. There are a number of anomalies in this story, not least the fact that Kilve is a long way from Street.

Fossils of other Ichthyosaurs have been found at both Kilve and Street, and at Kilve they are found in the rocks known as Blue Lias, hence the name given to this dragon. Further 'place name' evidence is supplied by the fact that one of the headlands at Kilve is called Blue Ben.

The county museum at Taunton has a number of fossil Ichthosaurs, many found in the nineteenth century, but there are no records of this story. According to Simpson in her *British Dragons* (1980), it appeared in 'a recent folklore collection'. Putsham Hill lies just to the south of Kilve, by the hamlet of Putsham, although this name is only now found on old maps.

The Tale of Blue Ben

There was once a great fire-breathing dragon called Blue Ben who lived inside Putsham Hill near Kilve. Blue Ben was friendly with the Devil and occasionally the Devil would take Blue Ben down to hell to pull his chariot when he did a tour of his infernal kingdom. One day Blue Ben had got very hot, as happens to all fire breathing dragons, and he went down to the sea to cool himself down, but got stuck in the sticky mud on the seashore, could not free himself and so drowned when the tide came in.

The Kingston St Mary Dragon

Dragon tales are well established in this region and the church at Kingston St Mary has dragon carvings on its tower, a type known as Hunky Punk dragons, and on the church of St Mary at Bishops Lydeard, a village only three miles (4.8 km) to the west, there is a fine carving of a dragon on the right side of the north face of the tower depicting a dragon with a stone lodged in its mouth, a feature probably inspired by this legend which is well known in the locality.

The beach at Kilve where the dragon called Blue Ben drowned when it got stuck in the mud.

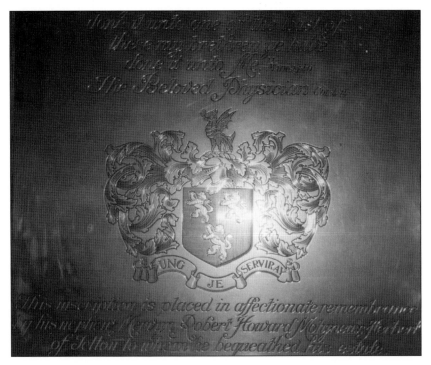

The memorial of the Herbert family in St Mary's church, Kingston St Mary, showing a wyvern used as a crest on the coat of arms.

Monuments to the Herbert family in the church and churchyard show them to have used a wyvern as their crest. Tetton House, near Kingston St Mary, was a secondary home of Lord Carnarvon, whose family name is Herbert. An heiress of the Acland family married the second Lord Carnavon (1774-1808), and it was the younger sons who occupied the property and were buried in the church. The Carnarvon (Herbert) crest consists of a wyvern with wings held upright and holding in its mouth a human hand!

Curiously, a lead plaque in the church recording the names of the two church wardens in 1777 also features a wyvern. This does not seem to be particularly associated with either of the church wardens named so it may just further indicate the interest in and knowledge of the local dragon story. The design looks like the crest from a coat of arms but it is too early in date to be associated with a member of the Herbert family so it may simply have been copied by the 'plumber' from an heraldic source.

The weather vane on the village hall, just down the road from the church, also commemorates the story by taking the form of a dragon.

The story below was recorded in 1911 from local harvesters and a maid servant. The person who recorded it was shown the very place in Ivyton Lane where the stone is reputed to have come from. On the 1905 Ordinance Survey map, which was surveyed in 1886, there is the word 'stone' shown near the road from Kingston St Mary to the small hamlet of Ivyton, suggesting that an ancient stone monument, or perhaps another notable stone, stood there. Could this be the spot where the story says this dragon met its end? Unfortunately, there is no stone to be seen on the spot today and no-one locally can be found who recalls a stone being there.

The Tale of the Kingston St Mary Dragon

There once was a terrible dragon that lived at Kingston St Mary. It breathed out great flames, which it used to cook its meat, whether animal or human. However, this meant that no-one could get near enough to kill it and it gave great problems to all the people of the village. But there was a clever villager who, one day, had an idea for a way of defeating the dragon. He climbed

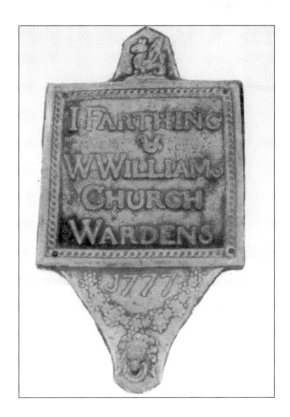

A lead plaque featuring a wyvern, dated 1777, in St Mary's church, Kingston St Mary.

The Kingston St Mary dragon on a weather vane on the village hall.

up the lane by Ivyton to the brow of the hill where there stood a huge rock at that time. The hill was very steep and this rock stood right on the brow of the hill. This man, whose name is now forgotten, stood behind the rock and waited for the dragon to appear. Eventually it did so and when it was at the base of the hill he gave a great shout. This caused the dragon to look up and when it saw the villager it opened its mouth to let forth a great spurt of flame to destroy this insolent person who had dared to shout at it. At that moment the villager gave the rock a great shove with his shoulder and it began to move. It rolled faster and faster down the hill and straight into the dragon's open mouth. There it lodged fast, choking the dragon until it died, to the great relief of all the villagers.

The Dragon of Norton Fitzwarren

Norton Fitzwarren is situated two and a half miles west of Taunton and this story, obviously of ancient origin, has a number of interesting aspects. The dragon lived in an Iron Age hill fort that, according to a local belief, was the site of the main settlement in the area at one time. This is enshrined in a local rhyme, 'Taunton was a furzy down, when Norton was a thriving town.'

There is evidence that there was Saxon occupation of the hill fort and the emblem of the Saxons was a dragon. So was the fierce battle between

Saxons and native Britons? The *Anglo Saxon Chronicle* says that the Saxon leader Centwine was fighting the Britons in West Somerset in 682. If so the Saxons may have occupied the hill fort as an easily defended position and emerged from time to time to raid the nearby villages and hamlets. Bearing in mind that people remained in the same place for generations, this story could well be the interpretation of a memory of these Saxon raiders that has been passed down by local storytellers for over a thousand years.

This story is a rare example of a dragon tale that explains where the dragon came from. In this case it was created by a spontaneous process, in keeping with a theory prevalent until the late seventeenth century that some animals were 'generated' from rotting flesh and, in the case of dragons, great hatred. This idea is mentioned by Edward Topsell in *The Historie of Serpents*, 1608: 'For they say that as Bees are generated out of the body of Oxen, and Drones of Horses, and Hornets of Asses: so do the bodies of men ingender out of their marrow a Serpent, and for this cause the Ancients were moved to consecrate the Dragon to Noble-spirited men'.

Fulke Fitzwarin, who is credited with slaying this dragon, is a historical character, but there were seven successive men of that name in the family. The first quarelled with King John and was exiled abroad but pardoned in 1203. He held lands in Shropshire, but not apparently in Somerset. However, the fifth Fulke Fitzwarin did have estates in Somerset in around 1380. There are still members of the Fitzwarren family today and some branches incorporate a dragon in the form of a wyvern, with wings extended, on their crest and as part of their coat of arms. This may be an example of a 'charter legend' where a local family claimed an existing dragon story to explain how they came to hold their lands and why a dragon should appear on their arms. There are also clues that they hijacked a somewhat different version of the story that once existed and had a very ancient origin.

The Tale of Fulk Fitzwarin and the Norton Dragon

A dragon emerged from the old camp on top of Norton Hill after a fierce battle. There were piles of bodies lying around and the dragon arose from the rotting flesh. From time to time it came down from the hill and terrorized the surrounding countryside, causing great damage and loss of life. This continued until a local man, Fulk Fitzwarin, engaged the creature in battle, and after a fierce fight killed it. To mark this great battle Fulk Fitzwarin added the image of a dragon to his coat of arms.

There are clues in All Saints Church at Norton Fitzwarren that there was a different version of the Norton dragon story in existence in around

1500 and probably before this. In the church is a very fine rood screen, unlike other Somerset screens in style, although similar to one at Aldenham in Hertfordshire. The lower part resembles those found at Long Sutton and Chew Magna but the highly ornamented cornice may not have been carved by local carpenters.

The cornice has four bands of ornamentation, the first and third being vine leaves, the intermediate being water crowfoot, or a similar plant, and the lowest band which has a six inch (15 cm) high sequence of carved figures said to represent the story of the Norton Dragon. The screen dates from about 1500 and originally ran right across the width of the church but it has undergone a number of alterations since that time.

The carvings were originally brightly painted, but the screen was given a coat of oak paint in around 1825, after which the colours could barely be seen. The screen is believed to have been restored in 1870 when the carvings were cleaned and repainted, although the recolouring may also have occurred in another restoration that was carried out in around 1900.

It is remarkable that this fascinating carving has survived at all. The rood screen was dismantled and altered to fit the width of the chancel arch with a second part fitted across the arch of the north chapel. According to *The Church Times* in 1886 'when the church was defaced, at the time of the restoration, it was entirely taken down, and only put back by the energy of the present rector, and then against the advice of most of the neighbouring clergy. It was pieced together in an entirely different manner to the original in order to fit the new chancel arch....'.

During the time that the screen was dismantled the section containing the dragon carving was stolen from the church, but was later found by the rector in a curiosity shop in Taunton and was recovered and later replaced in the rood screen. The lower band of the cornice in the section now in the chancel arch shows a dragon story which is said to be the battle with the Norton dragon, but seems to tell a different version to the one known locally today. In this very fine and spirited carving there is no knightly figure, as would be expected if Fulk Fitzwarin was featured, but it seems to show local people dealing with the monster but presents problems of interpretation.

The Dragon Story Carving:

All the figures or scenes are on a gold painted vine leaf background (plates III).

Scene 1. First come three dogs, all wearing gold collars, running away to the left, the first of these, which is the largest dog and painted a dark colour, is a greyhound type; while the next is a smaller, reddish brown hound and the third is dark in colour and also a hound. They all appear to be fleeing from the scene.

Scene 2. Next is a man in a gold tunic with turned back cuffs, a broad black belt, Elizabethan style hat, brown socks and dark shoes. He is facing towards a dragon and holds something like a hoop in his left hand and what appears to be a bottle in his right hand.

Scene 3. The next part depicts a dragon, facing towards the man with the hoop, its mouth opened wide to display its teeth. It is dark in colour except for the prominent gold vertebrae or square spines along its back. It has four legs, with feet having three sharp claws. The tail, which is long, is looped back over itself.

Scene 4. Behind the dragon is a bowman, facing away from the monster. He wears a reddish brown tunic with a broad gold belt, black hose and gold shoes. He holds a bow in his left hand, the string suggesting that the arrow has just been loosed. He is facing towards three plough oxen.

Scene 5a. Next are three oxen, a dark one with no horns, a brown one and a red one with horns, all wearing ox collars or yokes, painted gold, and joined to each other with a twisted rope. The ox driver, holding a long rod, has his mouth open to urge them on. The plough is of simple design, widely used in Norman England in the eleventh and twelfth century but shows none of the improvements

The Norton Fitzwarren rood screen (c. 1500) with a dragon story carved on it.

The dragon story carving, Norton Fitzwarren: scene 9.

that were made in the design of the plough from the fourteenth century onwards.

Scene 5b. The ploughman holds the plough in both hands and wears a gold tunic with gold hose and shoes, and a dark hat. The left leg of his hose is reddish, while the right is dark.

Scene 6. Behind the ploughman comes a man with a red tunic, the right leg of his hose being reddish in colour and the right dark. He holds a device used to spread seed on the fields.

Scene 7. The next scene shows a naked man, his penis clearly shown, with hands together in an attitude of prayer, being swallowed by a dragon, who has consumed his legs as far as his knees. The man's head is turned slightly to the right and his pink tongue is protruding from his mouth. The dragon, painted black with clearly marked scales, is an elongated creature with a long neck and long looped blunt ended tail. Its head has upright ears and it looks almost like a panther; it has four feet, the front two having claws, while the rear two have cloven hooves.

Scene 8. Behind the dragon the words 'Ralphe Harris C W' appear in raised, 'gothic' lettering.

Scene 9. (see above) Following the lettering, a naked male figure with curly hair holds what seems to be a musical instrument to his lips and this is 'directed' at two naked female figures, each of whom grasps a lock of the others hair in one hand and holds what appears to be a length of rope in the other. Behind the figures are large vine leaves like those that immediately precede the first scene in the carving.

This is one of the finest and most intriguing carvings of a dragon story to be found in Somerset but it is impossible to be sure what it depicts. Two dragon stories were known in the district and this one probably predates the one told above involving Fulk Fitzwarin and first documented in the late nineteenth century. The second version of the story is mentioned in the *Proceedings of the Somerset Archaeological Society* in 1851, 'Popular tradition says it [the camp] was once the haunt of a fierce and gigantic serpent, which having been generated from the corruption of many dead bodies which lay there, spread terror and death through the neighbourhood'. It is referred to again in the *Proceedings* in 1872 and this is more descriptive of what may be happening in the carving. 'According to the legend, the dragon who lived on the hill seemed to have infested the fields where the ploughmen were, and here he was in pursuit of the men'. The story was obviously well known in the area but the reference is so brief since probably all the locals knew the story anyway!

During the dismantling and re-erection to fit a different space it is possible that part of the screen's story has been lost. It would have been necessary to remove about six feet (2 m) from the screen to fit it in its new position and while logically a section other than the one that contains the dragon story would have been removed it cannot be assumed that this was the case. The dragon story carving occupies the whole width of the chancel arch and if the original story carving was of a greater length it would have been necessary to discard one or more sections to fit it into the space. The story may also have been reassembled in a different order, a suggestion first made in 1886. If either or both of these was the case then it would not be surprising to find that interpretation of the story is now very difficult.

Examination of the carving reveals that the first and last sections are in their correct positions as they precede and end with carvings of large leaves, respectively, to indicate the start and the end of the story.

At first glance it might be assumed that each scene illustrates a different part of a continuous story like a cartoon, however, it is strange that the two dragons shown are so different. If one story, it would be expected that the dragons would be identical to show that the same creature was shown in two scenes but engaged in different activities. Could it be that there were two dragons in this story?

The following is offered as a tentative interpretation:

Scene One: Three dogs appear to be fleeing rapidly from the spot where their master is confronting a dragon. They may be hunting dogs that helped their master to track down the dragon but turned and fled when it appeared, leaving him to tackle it alone.

Scene Two: A man faces a dragon. In his left hand he holds a hoop-like device to put round its jaws to stop it biting him, while the bottle in his right hand may contain a poison with which to kill or disable the monster. In many British dragon stories, slayers who are of a more humble class than knights often use natural guile to defeat the creatures.

Scene Three: This is the fearsome dragon that is terrorising the area. The body of this monster is very much like that of a crocodile or alligator except for the head and is unlike any other dragons found in Somerset. Could the carver have seen a crocodile or an illustration of one as his inspiration? In some parts of Britain stuffed crocodiles were to be seen hanging up in apothecaries' shops who sometimes claimed they were the bodies of dragons.

Scene Four: The bowman, who seems to have just released his arrow, is curiously facing away from the first dragon and towards the oxen. This scene is on a separate piece of wood and could well be out of place. Close examination of the whole carving has not shown any sign of the arrow. His whole attitude is that of a hunter rather than someone fleeing from the dragon behind him. This scene does not seem to fit into any other part of the existing carving, suggesting it is related to one or more scenes no longer present.

Scenes Five and Six: The ploughman and the oxen are probably representative of peaceful rural life, the sort of everyday activity that was suffering from the depredations of a dragon.

Scene Seven: A second dragon is devouring a naked man. His attitude would indicate that he is fully reconciled to his fate, and is a sacrificial victim, a fact further suggested by his being naked. While most people tend to associate young maidens with sacrifices to dragons, in fact, males are more commonly depicted in Somerset. The second dragon is quite different to the first one and a very unusual depiction, having claws on its front feet and cloven hooves on its back ones. Could the presence of hooves indicate that this one represents the Devil?

Scene Eight: The name 'Ralphe Harris' is almost certainly the name of the churchwarden at the time and that may be what the following letters, 'C W', stand for. Ralphe Harris was buried at the west end of the church in 1509. It is unusual for the name of a churchwarden to appear on carved work at this early date.

Scene Nine: A naked male figure holds a tube to his mouth that looks like a musical instrument. However, it may be the tube is something else – a sort of pea shooter? It is apparently being aimed at the rear of one of the two naked females so it may represent a fertility ritual of some sort. The two female figures are pulling at each other's hair with one hand

and hold a piece of rope in their other. Nothing else like this is known in the county or indeed anywhere elsewhere. The whole of this scene is a mystery. Perhaps, though, it was this scene that led to the parishioners seeking its removal from view in the nineteenth century!

There are some alternative interpretations: In 1872 it was suggested that the scenes were allegorical of ones of sloth and industry, virtue and vice. However, it is hard to see this allegory in the carved story. In 1908 it was suggested that the Norton carving illustrated the story of the Dragon of Rhodes. This incident is supposed to have occurred in 1349 with a dragon having a long neck and a serpent's head tipped with mule's ears, four feet with claws like a bear, tail like a crocodile, and a body covered in hard scales. It also had wings, which neither of the Norton dragons possesses. In this story a knight, Gozione, purchases a horse and two courageous, English hunting dogs and trains his servants to hold the dragon by clamping its jaws and twisting the tail using cords to hold it while it's attacked. He then proceeded to the Island of Rhodes where he used the dogs to hunt the dragon and eventually, after exhausting the creature, his servants rushed forward and as instructed secured it with ropes.

A dragon legend from Brent Pelham in Hertfordshire has some similar aspects to the Norton carving. Piers Shonks, a giant, was out hunting one day with his three hounds when he encountered a terrible dragon and killed it by shooting it with an arrow. Other aspects of the story, however, do not seem to fit.

The Great Worm of Shervage Wood

Shervage Wood is on the northern edge of the Quantock Hills, twelve miles (19.3) km from Minehead. An ancient hill fort is situated nearby, but used to be in this wood as it was once of much greater extent then at present. In the church at Crowcombe, mentioned in this tale, is a carved bench end depicting two people attacking a double headed dragon (plate IX). Could this be an indication that there was a medieval or earlier legend of a dragon in the area, and this tale, recorded in the early twentieth century, was the remnants of an earlier story now much altered from the original?

The hill fort where the dragon was supposed to have lived can still be found in the woods and another interesting aspect of this tale is that it describes how one part of the dragon ran to Bilbrook, some eight miles away from the wood. At Bilbrook is to be found an old inn, now a pub, restaurant and hotel called The Dragon House, but formerly the Green Dragon Inn. Nearby is a stone cross bearing a large bronze sword by a cross roads, and this is known locally as 'Dragon Cross' and is believed to be sited at the point the dragon, or at least the half that ran in this direction, died in its attempt to reach the sea.

There are two versions of this story, and the first one below was told by a storyteller from the village of Nether Stowey. As originally told it was in the Somerset dialect, (see Appendix 1 as an example of how most of these local stories would have sounded when being presented to listeners at the beginning of the twentieth century and earlier).

The Tale of the Great Worm of Shervage Wood

This 'great vurm' a huge, serpent-like creature lived in the wood on the site of a prehistoric hill fort. It spent most of the day asleep with its huge body coiled around a tree growing in the old camp. The monster was said to be as thick as three oak trees and, when it could, ate any humans it was able to catch. It was well known to have eaten a shepherd and two other men who had gone too near its lair and were never seen again. It would come out of the wood, crush sheep or cattle and then swallow them whole before going back to sleep to digest its meal. Even the wild ponies that grazed quietly among the trees would mysteriously disappear, much to the anger of the local farmers who were then prevented from selling them at Bridgwater Fair.

Gradually food for the 'great vurm' began to run out as all the woodland ponies were used up, and the farmers carefully guarded their remaining animals on the lower slopes. It was said that even the deer and rabbits fled to Hurley Beacon, a nearby hill.

All the local inhabitants were scared and none dared to come within a mile of the wood. This was particularly hard for those who made a living there and among these was an old women who lived in Crowcombe, a village at the foot of the Quantocks some two miles (3.2 km) from the wood.

During the late summer she earned a little money by picking worts, (whortleberrie, bilberries) which she made into tarts and sold at the nearby Triscombe Fair. She was very upset at the thought of all that fruit going to waste and how she was losing the chance to earn some money. Then one day a man from Stogumber arrived at Crowcombe. Stogumber is only three miles (4.8 km) away, but in those days people did not travel so far afield as now, so he was regarded as a 'stranger'. This stranger was a woodman and he got talking to the old lady. She persuaded him to go up to Shervage Wood to look at the timber there and to see if the worts were ripe. He agreed to do so and she gave him a lunch of bread and cheese, along with some cider, to take with him. He was not familiar with the area and by the time he got to the wood, noticing a great many ripe worts on the way, it was already noon. He saw a log and decided to sit on it to eat his lunch.

No sooner had he begun to eat when the 'log' moved under him. He jumped up in alarm and realised it was a dragon. 'Hold a bit! cried the man and grabbed his axe. 'Thee do movey do thee? Then take that' bringing down his axe so hard he cut the monster clean in two, and both ends of the 'log' began to bleed.

One part of the dragon then ran as fast as it could to Bilbrook, eight miles (12.8 km) to the west, while the other part ran to Kingston St Mary, ten miles (16 km) to the south east. Since the two parts were separated and could not rejoin, the dragon died.

After the dragon had disappeared, the woodman finished his lunch and walked back down to Crowcombe, with a hat full of ripe worts that he had collected on the way. He found the old women and told her that there had been a dragon in the wood, but it had now gone. However, he was suspicious of her motives for sending him to the wood and questioned her about it. She replied 'Didn't 'ee know? Didn't someone tell 'ee?'. The tale finishes with the comment, which no doubt had great local significance, 'Her were a Crowcombe woman!'

Kingston St Mary, a village three miles (4.8 km) north of Taunton and the destination of one half of the 'vurm', also has its own dragon legend (see p. 85). Perhaps this half survived long enough to give rise to a new story!

The ditch surrounding the hill fort at Shervage Wood where a dragon is supposed to have lived.

The Tale of the Great Worm of Shervage Wood: a second version

This was a long dragon, of the type they call a worm, and it devoured every living thing within reach. Because of this the local woodman was unable to go to the wood and cut the faggots on which his livelihood depended.

At last starvation made him desperate and drove him to work at a time when he thought the dragon had gone elsewhere in search of prey. All that morning he cut wood unmolested, seeing and hearing nothing of the monster. At noon he sat on a fallen log, half buried in the ferns, to eat his 'nummit (noon-meat). As he sat, the log suddenly heaved and squirmed under him, so he jumped up and cried 'So thee do movey, do 'ee? Take that then!'. He then struck his axe into the creature, turned and fled from the wood. But what became of the dragon afterwards no man knows, for it was never seen again!

The Human-Headed Dragon of Wells

The cathedral at Wells is believed to date back to the Time of Ine, King of the West Saxons, who founded a minster church there around 705. Since then it has been rebuilt and added to many times over the centuries. Jocelyn was Bishop of Bath between 1206 and his death in 1242, the title Bishop of Bath and Wells was not to be used until some time later. He was the son of Edmund of Wells who held an estate at Wellesleigh and had a house in the city. His elder brother Hugh was archdeacon at Wells and later Bishop of Lincoln. Both were friends of King John and acted as his advisors, although quite often the King did not follow their advice. On one occasion the King quarrelled over the choice of an archbishop of Canterbury with the Pope, and would not allow the new archbishop to land in England.

The Pope put the country under an edict in 1208 which meant that all the churches were closed and services suspended, and then excommunicated the King. Jocelyn, Hugh and four other bishops then went to France in voluntary exile. It was during this period abroad that Jocelyn acquired a magnificent gilt and enamelled crozier depicting St Michael fighting a dragon and decorated with other dragons, from Limoges (plate VI).

The King finally gave in to the Pope's wishes in 1213 and Jocelyn and the other bishops returned to England. Was it when he returned with his magnificent 'dragon crozier' that the legend began that he had killed a dragon or perhaps it arose after his death, even though it actually depicts St Michael slaying a dragon.

I *George and the dragon on a notice board outside St George's church, Dunster.*

II *A Saxon carving of a dragon slayer from St Mary the Virgin church, East Stoke, illustrating a local folk tale that was probably related to the dragon incident in the early English poem* Beowulf.

III   *The dragon story carving, Norton Fitzwarren: scene 1* (top); *scenes 2, 3 and 4* (middle);
scene 5a (bottom).

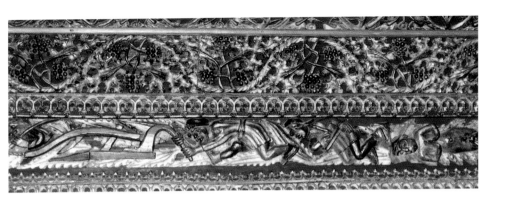

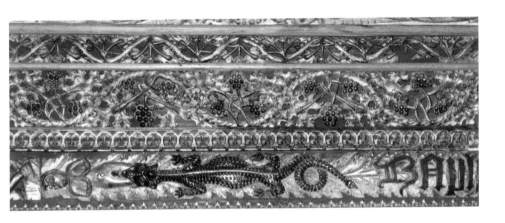

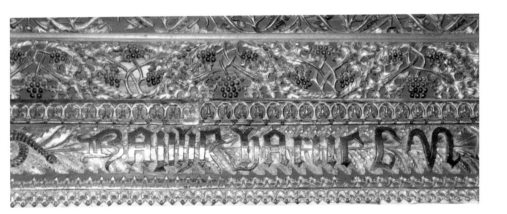

The dragon story carving, Norton Fitwarren: scenes 5(b) and 6 (top); scene 7 (middle); scene 8 (bottom).

IV   *Inn sign of the George and Pilgrim Hotel at Glastonbury showing St George holding the sword which, according to a local legend, he was given by the abbot.*

V   *St Andrew's church, Wiveliscombe, before the rebuilding of 1827. The crack that necessitated this work is clearly shown in this contemporary painting. It was apparently this work that caused the devil to appear riding on a green dragon.*

VI *The crozier of Bishop Jocelyn, featuring St Michael fighting the dragon and decorated with other dragons, which he brought back from Limoges in 1213.*

VII *A Hunky Punk dragon on St Martin's church, Worle.*

XII *St George and the dragon on a bench end at St George's church, Dunster.*

Opposite page
Top left: VIII *Two Amphisbaena dragons on a bench end at St Peter and St Paul's church, Churchstanton.*
Top Right: IX *A two-headed dragon in battle on a bench end at The Holy Ghost church, Crowcombe.*
Bottom left: X *A dragon's head, a vine and two birds carved on a bench end at The Holy Ghost church, Crowcombe.*
Bottom Right: XI *A bench end carving with a dragon's head in the lower left corner of the central panel at The Holy Ghost church, Crowcombe. The top panel shows two 'Green Men'.*

XIII *A dragon
preening its wing on a
carved bench end
St Michael's church,
North Cadbury.*

Opposite page: XIV *A very rare type of dragon, the Hominoida chlorodraco, shown on stained
glass in a window at St John the Baptist church, Glastonbury.*

XV   *An eleventh-century carving of a pair of fighting cockatrice, All Saints church, Lullington.*

XVI   *A kneeler decorated with a fire-breathing dragon, St Mary the Virgin church, Isle Abbots.*

XVII   *Door handles made in 2000 in the form of stylized Celtic dragons on the inner doors of St Barnabas church, Queen Camel.*

XVIII   *Somerset's present coat of arms on a magnificent stone carving above the main entrance to County Hall, Taunton.*

XIX *The Somerset dragon on a tapestry made by Candice Bahowth in 1989, County Hall, Taunton.*

XX *Dragons supporting statues of St Mary and St John in St Pancras church, West Bagborough.*

XXI *St George on a stained glass window in St Michael's church, Milverton.*

XXII   *A medieval carving of St George on a pillar behind the pulpit in St Decumen's church, St Decumen.*

XXIII *St Margaret* (left) *and St Michael* (right) *on a fifteenth-century stained-glass window in All Saints church, Trull.*

XXIV *A misunderstood dragon? The Minehead Sailer's Horse making its annual appearance in May 2000.*

XXV   *The Revd Nigel Done, playing the part of the dragon slayer Bishop Jocelyn of Wells, 'kills' the Worminster dragon during the childrens play at Dinder in November 2001.*

XXVI   *A mosaic, designed by Kate Rattray and made by children and the villagers of Dinder, Dulcote and North Wootton, is placed on the lawn near the Bishops Palace at Wells as a permanent reminder of the Worminster Dragon Play, held every fifty years.*

There is another 'dragon connection' with Bishop Jocelyn. The patronage of a church at Hinton, a village twenty-two miles (35 km) south of Bath, was given to Bishop Jocelyn about 1220. It seems that this is also the same time the church was dedicated, or an earlier dedication altered, to St George, a very popular saint at that time, but also a well-known dragon slayer!

Yet another connection with Bishop Jocelyn's dragon is said locally to be the existence of the place name Worminster to the south east of Wells. One of the names in Somerset dialect for a dragon was 'worm'. However, place name authorities give a different and less exciting origin for the name (see p. 71).

There are three versions of the dragon story of varying dates. The earliest account of Bishop Jocelyn's encounter with a dragon is found in a manuscript by Ranulf Higden entitled *Polychronicon* (History of the World). He was a monk at St Werburgh's Abbey, Chester and died in 1364. The manuscript was housed at Witham Friary near Frome for a while but eventually ended up at Eton College.

This story is unusual among dragon legends because the monster is described as having a human face. Although rare it is not unique: the 'serpent' that tempted Eve was sometimes depicted as a dragon with the face of a human female in early medieval manuscripts and there are early

A French medieval woodcut showing dragons having the upper half of human women. Was Brother Ranulf, who described the human headed dragon of Wells, inspired by seeing similar illustrations?

illustrations of half human half dragon creatures, the human part always being depicted as female. The description below of it lurking in 'the park' probably refers to 'the countryside' near Wells. The original Latin text was translated by the Revd Peter Thorburn: He also slew a certain deadly serpent which lurked in the park near Wells; [it was] depicted as four-footed and winged, with a human face. He dispatched it by striking off its head, engaging it in single combat after dismissing his entire retinue. (*Hic eciam quendam mortiferum serpentem in parcio iuxta Wellys latitantem. Facie humana effigiatum. Quadrupendem. Alatum. Caput amputando; percussit. Solus eum aggrediens abiectis a se familiaribus cunctis.*)

A somewhat later version of the story tells us that the dragon had a liking for eating children. This is quite rare. In some tales an agreement was reached with a dragon that if it left an area alone then a young maiden or young man was periodically offered to it as a sacrifice but children are not usually referred to.

Jocelyn was responsible for building the very impressive Bishop's Palace at Wells and, so the story goes, once fought a dragon. The terrible creature of this story had a liking for children. Bishop Jocelyn killed the dragon, took a knife and cut open its belly, whereupon the children it had swallowed jumped out unharmed. In the city of Wells and the surrounding area the story of Bishop Jocelyn's encounter with the dragon is well known and indeed the legend is kept alive today. It is a local tradition that a play about the slaying of the dragon, also known as the Worminster Worm or Worminster Dragon, is performed every fifty years to prevent the dragon reappearing and devastating the villages of Dinder, Dulcote and North Wootton, all of which lie within a short distance of Wells. The play was performed locally in 1901, in 1951 it moved to London for the Festival of Britain and performed locally again in 2002 (a year late because of the restrictions caused by the foot and mouth outbreak in 2001 – luckily the dragon did not reappear!). The long intervals between performances usually ensure that the script is rewritten for each new performance. The 2001 play was written by William Wych in the style of a medieval Mumming Play and called *The Great Worm of Dulcote Hill*.

The Tale of the Great Worm of Dulcote Hill

Two peasants were talking, when suddenly a third, Eli, rushed up to them in a panic for he had seen the venomous worm, a dragon with the face of a woman! Upon hearing this news all three fled the place and reported the sighting to the Lord of the Manor. They told their tale to Squire Wootton, who heard them out and then decided to send some of his soldiers to put paid to the monster. The soldiers engaged it in battle but after a great fight they were defeated, only one soldier returning, leaving the dragon dangerously enraged.

The surviving soldier warned the squire that the villages in the area, Dinder, Dulcot and North Wootton, must be warned of the danger they were now in. This the Squire agreed to do but was in despair as he did not know how to rid them of the dragon. However, the soldier had an idea, and suggested that the squire send a message to Bishop Jocelyn at the nearby city of Wells to inform him of their desperate plight. The squire was doubtful, as he felt such an exalted official would not be concerned with the troubles of ordinary people.

However, a relation of the soldier, Simon, was a painter who had worked at the Bishop's Palace, and knew Bishop Jocylyn. So the squire sent for him and despatched him to Wells to seek help. Simon arrived at Wells and managed to get an audience with Bishop Jocelyn, and the Abbot of Glastonbury who was also present. Simon told them about the terrible dragon that was terrorizing the area and how the people needed help to defeat it. The bishop sent Simon back to the squire with a message to say he would help and that spear, sword or mace would defeat the dragon by God's good grace.

The Bishop and the Abbot discussed the problem and decided that Holy Water, used at other times to defeat dragons and evil creatures, was not the way to defeat this dragon and a weapon would be needed. The abbot announced that at the abbey in Glastonbury there was a sacred sword, housed there for many years, but of unknown origin. The abbot felt in his heart that this was the weapon with which to defeat the dragon.

Soon afterwards, the bishop, the abbot and some monks arrived at the manor house of the squire with the sacred sword from Glastonbury. The bishop questioned the witness Eli about the dragon, but Eli was overwhelmed by the grandeur of the people present, and so the account of the dragon sighting was told by a peasant to whom he had first told his tale. The surviving soldier also related his story and told how the dragon was now enraged following the attempt of the squire's men to kill it. The bishop asked the soldier to describe this monstrous dragon in more detail, which he did:

It had a monstrous, powerful tail
It's body covered o'er with scale.
It slithered, yet 'twas footed four, with dragons wings above,
And on its head a women's face, a face a man could love!
Yet when it's eyes on me did turn
I like as froze, my gut did churn.
A brother soldier then did lunge and slash
Struck dead was he, as monstrous tail did lash.
Fled I then my soul to save.

All the people offered to help the bishop fight the dragon but Jocelyn said that he had prayed hard and God had spoken to him and revealed that he alone must undertake the task of ridding the area of this evil. Bishop Jocelyn then went forth to a field where, in his vision, God had told him he would encounter the dragon. He called loudly for the dragon to come forth, upon which it appeared.

The dragon tried to tempt the bishop to look upon its face, which Jocelyn refused to do as he knew this would condemn his soul to hell. Using a shield to see the whereabouts of the dragon he wielded the sacred sword from Glastonbury and struck off the head of the dragon. In thanks to God for this great victory over the evil monster, Jocelyn vowed to establish a new church at Dinder where the blood of the dragon was spilt, so cleansing the spot; to improve and extend the minster church at Wells and turn it into a cathedral and to return control and jurisdiction of the great abbey at Glastonbury to the abbot, powers that had been removed by Jocelyn's predecessor. All these things were done.

During the 2001 celebrations many other dragon-related activities took place in the villages and in Wells. These began on 30 June with a reading of *The Ballad of Bishop Jocelyn and the Dragon of Worminster Sleight* by its author, Christopher Somerville, a descendent of John Somerville who, legend has it, slayed the dragon known as the Linton Worm in 1174.

In July of that year a traditional skittles match was held between teams from the villages of Croscombe, Dinder/Dulcote, North Wootton and Pilton, the winning team to hold the Dragon trophy until the next match in 2051! The annual flower show in September had a dragon theme and a Dragon Dinner was held in the village hall with guest speaker the Rt Revd Jim Thompson, Bishop of Bath and Wells and spiritual descendent of the dragon slayer, Jocelyn.

October saw a dragon play performed by young people from local schools and an exhibition about the dragon festival and a reunion of those who took part in the 1951 event. At the end of October artist Dee Moxam organized a workshop in the village to build a forty-five feet long dragon in five portable sections. A great many people of all ages from the three villages spent six days building the dragon which was made of coloured tissue paper on a wire and wicker frame.

In November children saw the curate, Nigel Done, play the part of Bishop Jocelyn, suitably attired and mounted on a bike, attack the dragon built by the villagers with an eight feet long lance to 'save the children of the three villages'. The dying dragon bled not blood but sweets into the hands of the appreciative children! (plate XXV) After this the dragon was put on the lawn of Dinder House and lit from within with candles, providing an amazing and impressive sight. (see page 102)

On 30 December a 'Slaying the Dragon Service' was held at St Michael and All Angels church, Dinder, in which the Revd David Osborn gave a dragon-themed sermon with extracts from the dragon incident described in the poem *Beowulf*. He spoke about dragons and their characteristics such as anger, acquisitiveness, selfishness and hoarding instinct as applied to society today. Outside the church the five sections of the festival dragon were placed and lit from within by candles making an impressive and strange sight. The dragon made one final appearance when it was burnt on the New Year's Eve bonfire at North Wootton.

Another part of the celebrations included the construction of a mosaic designed by Kate Rattray and made by local children. This was placed on the lawn near the Bishops Palace in Wells on 5 February 2002 (plate XXVI) and a tapestry, made by Mary Stripp, was hung in Wells Museum while a living willow dragon sculpture was planted in the village of Dulcote later that year.

It is to be hoped that the mosaic and tapestry will act as permanent reminders to local people of the need to hold the festival every fifty years. The festival was almost lost in the twentieth century, only saved because of a chance remark by one old lady in the village, Peggy Portnell, who remarked that it was nearly time for the next dragon play. Up to that point most of the other villagers had not heard about it. Unfortunately she died just before the 2001/02 celebrations took place.

The Devils Dragon of Wiveliscombe

Located to the north west of Wellington and below the Brendon Hills, is the former market town of Wiveliscombe. The church, dedicated to St Andrew, was certainly in existence by the twelfth century and was rebuilt in the fourteenth century. However, in the nineteenth century a large crack appeared in the tower and the parishioners decided to rebuild the whole church, which they did between 1827 and 1829 (plate V).

This story, which is obviously of relatively recent date when compared with other Somerset dragon legends, was probably devised to make a good tale to tell in the local inns or told by parents when the children were gathered in front of the parlour fire at home. The tale of the Devil throwing rocks at churches is not unique to Wiveliscombe, as it was claimed that the Devil threw three huge rocks at Staple Fitzpaine church from the hill fort called Castle Neroche. Fortunately they all fell short, and at least one can still be seen in a field today!

Above the altar is a very fine rose window, whose central panel shows St Michael defeating the dragon. This monster is unusual in having two heads, both of which wear crowns. To one side of this scene is a Welsh

After 'Bishop Jocelyn' had slain the Worminster dragon it was placed on the lawn of Dinder House and lighted candles placed inside it to provide an impressive and eerie decoration.

dragon, and this also appears in another stained glass window that depicts St David of Wales.

The Tale of the Devil's Dragon at Wiveliscombe

It is said that in the year 1827, when the church was being rebuilt, the Devil suddenly appeared riding on a green dragon. He was very angry that the church was being enlarged and improved so began to throw huge rocks at the church in an effort to destroy it. However, the Devil was not a very good shot and missed the church, but before he could improve his aim St Andrew appeared and held up his cross before the Devil. Then both he and his green dragon fled and the church has remained safe and free from further attack to this day.

9

Bench End Dragons

Fortunately for us today, the medieval clergy allowed the use of symbols, emblems and illustrative scenes in their churches. These had a significant and well understood meaning to people at the time, although not all of these are clear to us today. The most notable and detailed examples are to be found in the magnificent carved bench (pew) ends to be found in many Somerset churches. These are often magnificent pieces of carving and some of the best examples are to be found in the western part of the county.

Most of these benches were installed in the fifteenth and sixteenth centuries providing seating for some members of the congregation for the first time. Until then congregations had merely stood in the open space that was the body of the church.

The county had grown rich on the wool trade, which was at its zenith at the time these benches were commissioned, and so the churches were able to afford to spend money on decorating the interiors including new seating. A number of local woodcarvers were very skilled craftsmen. Being local, the carvers well understood the interests of the people, particularly in such matters as the harvest that was so important to them in this very rural area, but also their superstitions and folk beliefs and the way they liked religious subjects to be depicted. As would be expected, many of the carvings are related to nature, featuring a range of both wild and domestic animals, foliage, a fairly large number of 'green men' - a representation of a nature spirit of very great antiquity, scenes from everyday life, with some coats of arms and heraldic animals.

Most of the Somerset bench ends were produced over a period of about a hundred years, but the names of only two of the woodcarvers are known to us. Simon Warman and a man known only as Gloss, can be identified by their initials or names and by distinctive characteristics in their carving. Other carvers, whose names are not known to us, can also be detected by distinctive elements in their work.

Among these carvings are a number of dragons, sometimes portrayed symbolically and with varying degrees of quality, but all of interest to the 'dragon hunter'. A representative selection of these medieval carvings is included here, but there are others to be found.

While the majority of the Somerset bench end carvings date to the fifteenth or sixteenth century, there are some of a much more recent date. The most notable of these are the fine bench end carvings produced in 1876 for St George's church at Dunster which depict representations of St George and St Michael slaying dragons. A series of bench ends in Halse church were all carved by local villagers in 1900, while a post-1912 bench end in St Andrew's, Old Cleeve, shows the modern coat of Arms of Somerset, the Wessex dragon holding a mace. These later bench end carvings form part of a long Somerset tradition and many are of very fine craftsmanship, quite equal to those made four hundred years earlier.

Alford's Man Eating Dragon

Alford is a small village, its stone cottages set in flat countryside west of Castle Cary. The name is derived from 'Ealdgyth's ford', and by 1086 was known as Aldedeford. The church is situated north of the village and stands beside the River Brue. All Saints church is built of the local lias stone and is in the Perpendicular style (1375–1550). It escaped restoration by the Victorians and has a nice little tower topped with a small pyramid roof. It has a good set of carved bench ends, one of which shows a dragon. While a large number of dragon representations can be found in various places within Somerset, this is one of the few to show a man being devoured. Other examples can be found at Norton Fitzwarren and Brent Knoll.

The church also has a stained glass wyvern, black on a shield shape, about six inches (15 cm) high in one of the windows.

This church possesses a fine bench end carving of a traditional dragon, which is notable because it appears to represent a dragon eating a man. The dragon, which occupies three quarters of the panel, is lying on its back and is shown without feet, indicating it is a 'worm-type' monster. The body is covered with ring scales that encircle it and wings with three segments that are positioned halfway along the body. The head has an eye, prominent elongated ear, and an open mouth with castellated teeth from which its arrow – like tongue protrudes. It has a long tail that curves above the body and is looped in two places. Opposite the dragon's mouth is a man's head, wearing what appears to be a flat, Elizabethan-style hat.

The face, which is carefully carved, has the lips drawn back in a look of terror and there is no body, so perhaps this has already been eaten by the dragon!

A man-eating dragon carved on a bench end at All Saints church, Alford.

A wyvern on a stained glass window in All Saints church, Alford.

Bicknoller's Dragons

This pretty village has many thatched cottages of the sixteenth and seventeenth centuries and its name is derived from 'Bica's alder tree'. Its regular layout suggests a planned settlement probably dating from the eleventh century. The church, dedicated to St George, dates to the twelfth century, but only the font and south wall of the nave survive from this date. The chancel and tower date to an extensive rebuild in the fifteenth century, while the north aisle, north chapel and porch are of the early sixteenth century. There is a fine series of bench ends from around 1530 and some later ones too.

A bench end carving, dating to 1932, shows St George, mounted on a horse, wearing armour and shown with a halo, impaling a wyvern. This creature has a large head, its mouth is open to show sharp teeth and a forked tongue. It has a long snake-like body with ring scales and a crest running down the length of its back, terminating in a barbed tail. On a smaller panel below this scene is a shield bearing the cross of St George which is surrounded by circlet of roses.

*St George defeating a forked-tongue dragon on a bench end in
St George's church, Bicknoller.*

St George and the dragon in a niche on the porch of St George's church, Bicknoller.

On a screen in the church are a series of shields painted with different coats of arms and emblems. Among these is the red dragon of Wessex holding a mace on a gold background, which is the official arms of Somerset adopted in 1911. Next to this is a shield bearing the red cross of St George.

In a niche on the porch is a small statue of St George, probably dating from the 1930s and standing where an earlier statue of the saint probably stood. St George, wearing armour and a cloak, stands with an elongated shield in his left hand with the defeated dragon at his feet. This carving bears a very strong resemblance to the statue of St George in Florence by Donatello, and may have been based on this famous Italian image of the saint.

The Chedzoy Wyvern

Chedzoy is a small village on the Somerset Levels. The name is derived from 'Cedd's Island and a settlement is recorded as early as 729. It lies to the east of Bridgwater and below the Poldon Hills. A Roman villa was

A wyvern with ring scales on a bench end in St Mary's church, Chedzoy.

found here in the nineteenth century but its location has now been lost. The church, dedicated to St Mary, is situated in the centre of the village and has thirteenth century arcades flanking the nave and a chancel added later, but rebuilt in 1884-5. There are carved bench ends dating from the sixteenth century.

The bench end dragon at Chedzoy is of the early dragon types known heraldically as a Wyvern and is of the style used by the kings of Wessex. It faces to the right and has strong legs ending in fearsome claws. The body is covered with ring scales and there is a ridge along the back which continues down the tail. The head, on a short neck, has small ring scales, a tiny eye and a mouth open to reveal the teeth. Attached at its shoulders is a pair of curving wings. It has a long scaled tail which wraps around an heraldic style belt with a square buckle, which may suggest it was copied from part of a coat of arms. The initials 'S', 'W' and two 'I's are carved on the belt.

The south porch of the church bears three stone tablets, one of which shows it was built in 1579. Next to this is a tablet bearing the letters H.P., believed to stand for a member of the Pembroke family, and below these letters is a pair of weaver's combs and a wyvern – the badge of the family.

The Churchstanton Entwined Dragons

Churchstanton lies nine miles (14.4 km) south west of Taunton. The church, dedicated to St Peter and St Paul, is probably of Saxon or even earlier foundation. The chancel is thirteenth century, with major work carried out in the fifteenth and sixteenth century which saw the building of the south aisle, the south porch and the raising of the tower, with four fine gargoyles, to its present height, although the battlements were renewed in 1826. The interior was remodelled in 1830, when box pews replaced the earlier benches and some of the carved bench ends were incorporated into a gallery. One of these has a pair of dragons on it (plate VIII).

The bench end dates from the late fifteenth or early sixteenth century, and shows a pair of amphisbaena dragons, that is a monster having a head at both ends. These are twisted and entwined to form an attractive decorative feature, the upper head being the larger of the two.

The Cothelstone Armorial Wyvern

Cothelstone lies in the Quantock Hills and consists of just a few cottages, a farm, the manor house and the church. Its name is derived from 'Cuthwulf's settlement'. The church, to be found behind the manor house, is dedicated to St Thomas of Canterbury, and is mostly fifteenth century but of an earlier foundation. The manor belonged to

A wyvern on a coat of arms carved on a bench end at St Thomas of Canterbury church, Cothelstone.

the Stawell family from the twelfth century until 1790, when it passed to the Esdailes, and the church is full of monuments to members of both families.

Among the carved bench ends, dating from 1863, is one bearing the coat of arms of a member of the Esdaile family. This was carefully copied from the earlier bench ends that were replaced during the restoration at that time. This has a wyvern set on a central shield within the coat of arms, and is a good Somerset example of a Wyvern being used on the arms rather than as a crest.

A fine stained glass window above the altar, set up as a war memorial to 'Arthur James Esdaile, Frederick Lane Edwin and Sidney and Albert Welch who gave their lives in the Great war 1914–18', shows St Michael impaling a red dragon with a cross on an elongated shaft, along with St George who is spearing a green dragon with a jousting lance. Above the main scene are inset panels with devices from the Esdaile coat of arms, including a wyvern dragon, while their complete coat of arms, including a wyvern, can be seen in a corner of the window.

The Dragons of Crowcombe

Crowcombe is located below the western slopes of the Quantock Hills just off the Taunton to Minehead road (A 358). The name means 'Valley of the crows'. The manor is notable as having been passed down in the same family from the twelfth century to the present day. Crowcombe church, dedicated to The Holy Ghost, is built of local red sandstone. Its tower is fourteenth century and the rest of the church is mainly fifteenth century. In 1509 a Freemason from Exeter was paid thirty shillings for carving an image of 'Jorge' (St George) which was placed in a chapel of St George. In 1512 the records show that the 'whole cost of the Jorge', that is the cost of building and fitting out the chapel, was £27 11s 8d.

The church contains a superb series of carved bench ends dating from 1534, depicting a variety of subjects, including dragons. One of the most intriguing of these is a two-headed dragon. The meaning of this scene is open to several interpretations. It may represent a Biblical multi-headed dragon, or be a medieval depiction of the Devil with a second head borne on the abdomen, or it may represent some other paganistic belief. The dragon could represent the various perils that could befall the harvest and the nude figures may be the spirits of nature, who are battling to preserve the fertility of the crop from this 'evil'. However, Green Men are usually depicted as just heads and occur singly, so if these are intended to represent 'nature spirits' they are of an unusual form.

The fact that the vine springs from the mouth of what appears to be another dragon's head in the lower left hand corner of the panel is also interesting as there are many examples of carvings in churches that show foliage sprouting from the head of a green man, generally accepted as a symbol of fertility and regrowth, but in this case could it represent the 'rebirth' of the crop? In some cases dragons have been used in the past to represent rebirth, and dragon's heads with foliage springing from them occur on other bench ends in this church.

Alternatively could this be an attempt to illustrate the classical Greek myth of the Hydra? In this story Herakles, with the help of his servant Ioaus, fought and eventually killed a multi-headed dragon as one of the twelve 'labours' that he had to perform. Had the carver been told this classical Greek myth but did not have room to include the seven heads that the Hydra had? Perhaps it may illustrate a local legend, now forgotten, involving local people in combat with a monster.

There is also a double-headed dragon carved on a bench end at East Lyng, but in this case it seems to be giving forth the foliage from its mouth (see p. 119) while a single-headed dragon on a bench end at Hatch Beauchamp (see p. 121) also appears to give forth foliage.

In what is perhaps the most striking of these bench end carvings there is a dragon with a long pointed tail. A single leg and foot can be seen and a large wing fills the upper left hand corner of the panel. The monsters 'main' head, on the end of a long neck, is very ferocious looking, with a crest, prominent eye and a small, goat-like beard behind the lower jaw. Its mouth is open showing its teeth and a protruding tongue. The whole body is covered in scales. At the base of the neck, just forward of the shoulders is a second head with mouth open to show the teeth (plate IX).

The dragon seems to have sprung from behind a grape bearing vine, which is coming out of the mouth of a dragon whose head can be seen in the bottom left corner of the panel. The vine spreads out to fill the lower part of the panel. The dragon is being attacked by naked male figures, who are fighting it with staves, or possibly spears with the heads embedded in the dragon. One of the weapons is being thrust down the throat of the dragon's lower head and the second figure thrusts his weapon into the dragon's body just below it.

Below the main panel are two small panels, one of which also shows a dragon. This depicts just the front part showing the head with an eye and an ear and widely opened jaws. Two of its front feet can be seen and what looks like a back crest. In its open mouth another creature is apparent which appears to be a baby dragon! This would seem to be a live birth of a dragon and this baby has a very strong resemblance to the baby dragons hatching from scaly eggs on a carved bench end at North Cadbury church, even down to a mysterious 'neck crown' shown on both carvings (see p. 125). Some snakes have been observed regurgitating the remains of a meal and by extension the dragon, linked in the past with serpents, has been associated through this misunderstood habit with an old and widespread idea of 'rebirth' via the mouth. An alternative interpretation might be that it represents the consuming of another dragon since there are also legends about dragons growing to enormous sizes by feeding on other creatures of a poisonous nature (cf. the St Petroc stories).

In a second bench end (plate X) there is a vine that appears to be coming from the mouth of a dragon in the lower right hand corner of the panel. In the vine are two birds, one of whom is pecking at the fruit. It may be that in this case the dragon's head is actually in front of the vine, and this scene may be an interpretation of the legend of Peridexion that is shown very clearly in a carving at Hatch Beauchamp. This legend tells of a tree in India, here shown as a vine, that is pleasant, shady and full of fruit and in which doves live and feed. However, at the base of the tree lives a fearsome dragon that

The lower left panel of the dragon battle bench end possibly showing the live birth of a dragon at The Holy Ghost church, Crowcombe. The right hand panel appears to show a bat.

wishes to catch and eat them, but as long as the doves remain within the shadow of the tree they are safe. Those that venture outside the shadow are caught and devoured. When the shadow moves round to the left the dragon goes to the right, and vice versa, but the dragon is thwarted because the shadow never fails.

Another version of the tale gives it a Christian interpretation which explains its appearance on this bench end and the use of vines, common in Christian imagery, instead of a tree. In this version the vine represents God the Father, the fruit is the Son of God, while the shadow is the Holy Spirit and the dragon is the Devil. The moral is that all good Christians must keep within the shadow of the Holy Spirit and feed upon the fruit of God if they wish to remain safe from the wiles of the Devil.

In another carving (plate XI) there is a dragon's head from which foliage seems to spring. This bench end has three panels and this is from the centre panel. No two designs of bench ends in the building are the same and it seems that this is a variation of the other bench end described above showing a dragon and two birds and illustrates a story with a Christian meaning.

A fourth bench end shows yet another variation on the theme of the vine and dragons. In this case the creature's heads appear in the lower left hand corner and upper right hand corner of an elongated panel. Both have vines issuing from their mouths which entwine to fill the central area of the panel.

Dunster's Dragon Slayers

Dunster is a delightful little town, not a village as it is often described, which once had a busy port and was a successful trading centre. It is overlooked by a fairy tale castle, most of which dates from 1867-72, but its origins go back to Norman times and it is hard to believe the Saxons would not also have occupied such a good defensive site.

In the very old legend of the Carhampton dragon (see p. 78) St Carantoc led the creature to the stronghold of King Catho, which is generally identified as the place where Dunster Castle now stands overlooking the now drained Carhampton Marsh.

The church of St George is of ancient foundation since after the Norman Conquest in the eleventh century it was described as being 'rebuilt'. It was probably originally dedicated to a Celtic saint, now unknown, and the rededication to St George probably occurred when the cult of this saint became popular from the thirteenth century. In 1443 the Norman tower was replaced by the present one and between 1450 and 1500 the nave, eastern arm and south aisles were all rebuilt. In 1875

St Michael standing above a defeated dragon on a bench end at St George's church, Dunster.

St George slaying a wyvern
carved on the ambo at
St George's church, Dunster.

a complete restoration, costing £10,000, was undertaken under the direction of Mr G.E. Street, regarded as one of the most distinguished architects of his day.

The benches all have finely carved ends following a medieval tradition in this part of Somerset but were done in 1876 as part of the restoration work. Two of them represent dragon slaying saints, the one showing St George obviously being inspired by the medieval bench end featuring this scene in Hatch Beauchamp church.

The St George bench end carving: This shows a mounted St George thrusting his lance down the throat of a dragon with a mouth full of very sharp teeth, bat-like wings, four legs and a long, sinuous tail (plate XII).

The St Michael bench end carving: This is a very fine representation of St Michael standing on the body of the dragon, which has a large head, bat like wings with dots on them, four legs, two of which grip the calves of the saint, and a short tail. The saint, wearing armour and a crown, has a sword in his right hand which is held above his head, while his left hand holds a set of scales which he uses to weigh the souls of those cast into hell who might be deserving of saving. A head can be seen peeping out of each weighing pan, no doubt anxiously awaiting the verdict.

The most prominent representation in the church is a large carving of St George fighting a wyvern-type dragon which is to be seen on the front of the ambo - a 'walk in lectern'. The saint is on foot, thrusting the point of his sword into the back of the neck of the creature, which has its tail wrapped round his right leg. This was carved by a local craftsman, and bears the dedication: 'In thankfulness to God for the lives of Walter Bogue Bridges, Anne Caroline Bridges and Geoffrey Fownes Luttrell. Alys Luttrell had this fashioned 1958 '.

On the corner of the tower is carved a hunky punk dragon, looking outwards with typical, bat-like wings. The name board features a good representation, in colour and raised, of St George slaying the dragon. (plate I)

East Brent's Initial Dragon

This is an attractive village at the base of the large hill known as Brent Knoll. The church of St Mary is located at the western end of the village and has a tower that is capped by what has been described as one of the

An amphisbaena dragon entwined around the letter 'I' in St Mary's church, East Brent.

most elegant spires in Somerset. It used to be whitewashed to act as a marker to shipping on the Bristol Channel. Its fine set of carved benches date from the fifteenth century and are reputed to have been brought from Glastonbury Abbey when it was refurbished. An Amphisbaena, a dragon with a head at both ends, is depicted on one bench end in the way that such creatures were often depicted on medieval manuscripts. In this case the dragon is of the serpent type with both heads having prominent ears and eyes and is entwined around the letter 'I' forming the 'S' element of Ioannes Selwood, who was Abbot of Glastonbury from 1456–93. The monogram is set on a circular surround and is a particularly clear and bold carving.

East Lyng's Two-Faced Dragon

East Lyng is a village in the Somerset Levels to the east of Taunton on the A361. Its name comes from the Saxon word 'hlenc', which means hill. The church is dedicated to St Bartholomew and has fourteenth-century windows to the nave and chancel, the rest of the church is of the Perpendicular style (1375–1550). It has a good range of bench ends from the sixteenth and seventeenth centuries, one of which bears the date 1614. The tower of this church also has Hunky Punk dragons on it.

A carved bench end in East Lyng church has a curious dragon carving, which is open to at least two interpretations. It is either a two-headed dragon, an example of which can also be found at Crowcombe or, less likely, a person wearing a hat with a very strange and realistic dragon on it. The meaning of the carving is unclear, but one of the ways the Devil was sometimes depicted was as a dragon with a face in the abdomen and a serpent-like tail. This interpretation is given further credence since the dragon shown is also depicted with sexual organs, which is extremely rare in dragon representations. The dragon is a mixture of the traditional type with some unique characteristics. It has lightly flecked carving on the body which is probably meant to indicate scales. Its wings are scaly and folded against the body and attached close to the shoulder. The tail is long, curving upwards and behind the neck, while the two legs of the creature appear canine in nature but end in what seem to be webbed feet and between the legs are canine-like testicles. The dragon has a long neck with an open mouth from which issues foliage which curls upwards and branches outwards to fill the upper part of the panel. On the 'chest' of the dragon is a large, finely carved face looking downwards, but out of proportion to the main body of the creature.

An unusual, two-headed dragon on a bench end at St Bartholomew's church, East Lyng.

Halse's Sea Dragon

Halse is a small village with a church dedicated to St James. It is a plain church of local red sandstone with ham stone dressings dating back to the twelfth century. The font is of a similar date and it has a thirteenth-century tower that was altered in the fifteenth century when the nave, aisles and chapel were also rebuilt or added. One window contains Italian stained glass dated 1548.

The bench ends form a series which tell the story of the Biblical creation of the world as given in the first chapter of Genesis. All the bench ends are of a very high quality and were carved by parishioners who met in a cottage two evenings a week to undertake the carvings from 1900. They were designed by Grace Smith who had been to art school in London and the carving was directed by Mr Giles, a Master Carver from Taunton who visited the village once a week to advise and encourage the carvers.

One of these bench ends shows a fearsome dragon depicted rearing up with its fin-like wings extended, its angular head has a large eye and its

The Smith sisters who designed and helped carve the bench ends at St James's church, Halse. Grace, who designed the bench ends, is second from the left, and Janet, who carved the dragon, is fourth from the left.

mouth is open to reveal sharp teeth and a long tongue that terminates in an end like an arrow head. It has no legs, and its long body is covered with fine elongated scales and ends in a tail like that of a fish. This carving, by Janet Smith, illustrates the passage from Genesis 1:4 'And God saw the light, that it was good: and God divided the light from the darkness.' The dragon is used here to represent the darkness.

The Dragons of Hatch Beauchamp

Hatch Beauchamp is a small village now bypassed by the Taunton to Illminster Road (A 358). Its cottages line a single winding street that once formed the gateway, 'haecc' in Saxon, to the Royal forest of Neroche. The church, located behind Hatch Court, is dedicated to St John the Baptist and is almost all Perpendicular in style (1375–1550), except for the north chapel, south aisle, chancel and vestry that were added in the nineteenth century. The south doorway is dated 1530 which as also about the date of the carved bench ends. The church contains two dragon

*A sea dragon on a
bench end at
St James's church,
Halse.*

*A sixteenth-century carving of a dragon, a
tree and a bird on a bench end at St John
the Baptist church, Hatch Beauchamp.*

121

A sixteenth-century carving of St George and the dragon with another dragon on the lower panel of a bench end at St John the Baptist church, Hatch Beauchamp.

carvings, one of which is a very fine depiction of St George slaying the dragon, while the other illustrates a legend found in copies of the early medieval Book of Beasts, known as the Bestiary.

In the first is a dragon believed to have been carved by Simon Warman in the early sixteenth century. The dragon is crouching on the base of the panel with its forelegs flat on the ground and its hindquarters raised, but while the rear legs are shown the feet are out of sight. It has a long tail that hangs down between the legs and sweeps up the left side of the creature and over its back terminating in what appears to be a cleft, rope-like end. Its wings are of a traditional type, divided into four segments and, in this case, decorated with small circles, while the body is covered with small scales. The head, which is on a long neck, is twisted to look upwards, and an eye and ear are clearly shown as are square teeth in its open mouth. Above the dragon is a tree with foliage and berries which are being eaten by a bird, which will be keeping a close eye on the dragon below. This theme is reminiscent of scenes on the panels at Crowcombe.

A painting of St George and the dragon by Paolo Uccello (1396-1475) in the National Gallery, London shows a dragon with large roundels on its wings - yellow with green centres on the upper surface and red with green centres on the underside. Other examples of dragons with similar roundels are known.

The second dragon in the church, also probably carved by Simon Warman, is the standard scene of St George and the dragon, his horse rearing up above the cowering monster. The dragon is shown with its fore legs flat on the ground and its head turned upwards. Its mouth is open, but surprisingly no teeth are shown, although its eye and ear are clearly indicated. The body seems to be covered with small scales, and it has a very long tail that winds around the horses rear leg and forms a loop under its own body. The background to the scene shows a pattern of squared stones. This may be just a decorative device or it may represent a castle wall. St George is depicted as a medieval knight on horseback with helmet, full breastplate and leg armour. His right arm is raised to strike at the dragon with his sword which, according to Somerset legend, he got from Glastonbury Abbey (see p. 49).

The horse is shown with full medieval jousting regalia including a decorated crest, face piece and mane. Wide reins are attached to the bit; while the saddle, whose straps can be seen running over the rump and under the tail, has high back and front supports, and stirrups, the right foot of the Saint being in one. This medieval carving probably provided the inspiration for the carving on a nineteenth century bench end featuring the same scene in St George's church, Dunster.

Below the main panel there is a smaller one which also contains a dragon carving. This is a very much more fierce looking creature than the one being dealt with by St George above and is notable in having one very rare and one very unusual feature. This dragon has the same basic shape and form but is identifiable as a male and appears to be defecating!

There are several nineteenth-century carved bench ends in the church which copy the designs on the medieval ones. Among these are three copies of the 'dragon and tree' carving, and three of the St George and Dragon carving. None of these are up to the same standard as the earlier bench ends which were produced by a master carver.

The Dragons of North Cadbury

North Cadbury is one of Somerset's most attractive villages, located just north of the A 303, to the north east of Yeovil. Its name is derived from 'Cada's fort'. The church, dedicated to St Michael, is one of the finest Perpendicular churches (1375–1550) in England. It is plain outside, with the exception of its porches, the church being reconstructed around 1422. The tower was built by the rector John Feron who died in 1407. The series of carved bench ends date from 1538 and three of them have dragons on them.

One of the bench ends seems to show a very rare if not unique scene – the birth of dragons from eggs. Two wingless dragons are depicted, both having long necks and heads with pricked up ears and one has its mouth open. Both creatures appear to be emerging from scaly eggs. One of the dragons has what looks like a collar of leaves around its neck the significance of which is unknown. Very few legends mention the birth or creation of dragons, or even the fact that baby dragons existed. An alternative interpretation that has been offered is that these dragons are not coming from eggs but emerging from holes in the ground.

Another bench end shows St Margaret of Antioch emerging triumphant from the dragons back, after having been swallowed by him and before the end of her robe has entirely disappeared into the monsters jaws (p. 51). The story of St Margaret was widely known in the medieval period. It was said that while in prison awaiting martyrdom she prayed to see her adversary, the Devil, in some tangible form. Her prayer was granted, as a huge dragon appeared which opened its mouth and swallowed her. She made the sign of the cross in its belly, or some say, used her crucifix to cut her way out, and so demonstrated the power of Christ over the Devil.

The third dragon bench end at North Cadbury shows what appears to be a cockatrice, the most dangerous of all dragons. It stands on a pedestal which is ornately decorated with a floral foot. A thin leaf rises upwards

Two dragons apparently hatching from scaled eggs carved on a bench end at St Michael's church, North Cadbury.

from the left hand side of the pedestal and curls over the top of the creature. The body has elongated scales, most clearly seen on the neck and head, which resemble feathers, and a long tapering tail, the end of which rests on the pedestal. It has two legs, its left one resting on the pedestal and the right raised. The neck is turned back along the body with the head, which is beaked, has an eye but no visible ears, and a mouth that may be preening one of its wings, which curl upwards from the middle of the body (plate XIII), a habit that would be expected of a cockatrice.

Old Cleeve's Wessex Dragon

Old Cleeve lies between Minehead and Williton on the A39. The village is full of eighteenth- and nineteenth-century cottages, in the midst of which stands the parish church of St Andrew. Its chancel and south chapel

A modern Somerset dragon at St Andrew's church, Old Cleeve.

date from the thirteenth century, although there are indications that the church was originally Norman, of which only the north wall of the nave survives from the earlier building. The south aisle and south porch were added about 1450 and the tower was built in 1533. According to earlier accounts of the church interior it featured a dragon carving on the rood screen but the screen is no longer present, and according to a reference dated 1908 it had 'disappeared many years ago'. A book (1843) describes it '...the destruction of a dragon runs along, not only the Rood Screen, but the North Parclose also.' (see Bibliography: Neale, J.M., Webb, B.). However, there is still one dragon to be seen.

The church has a number of 'modern' bench ends, all well carved following a long Somerset tradition and one of these features the Wessex dragon as used on the official coat of arms of Somerset granted by the College of Heralds in 1911. Below it, on a ribbon, is the motto adopted by the county: *Sumorsaete Ealle*, which means 'All the people of Somerset'. The remainder of the panel is filled with curling acanthus leaves.

10

Hunky Punk Dragons

Many Somerset churches are decorated with carvings on the outside of towers and other parts of the building. Some of these are of mythical creatures and go back as far as the fourteenth century, such as the large dragons on the tower of All Saints church, Norton Fitzwarren, while others date from more recent times.

In some areas of England, including the West Country, these carvings are known as 'Hunky Punks' – the name probably derived from the old word 'hunker', meaning to squat, and 'punch' the name of a grotesque figure, now best known in the traditional Punch and Judy show. They are mostly non-functional features and should not be confused with gargoyles that are ornate water spouts.

A wide range of curious creatures are depicted, including dragons, and the observant dragon hunter will often be able to spot one or two, among the strange menagerie of animals represented. Probably these carvings were not only intended to serve a decorative function but were also to frighten away evil influences that may have wanted to enter the church. This is probably also the reason that some Somerset churches feature dragons on their porches, located either at the sides of the door or on each corner of the porch. A particularly good example of these can be seen at St Mary the Virgin, Isle Abbots. The porch is usually placed on the south side of the church, but in a number of cases carved dragons can be found on the north side of the building. As the north side of the church was believed to be 'unlucky' and under the control of evil spirits, the dragons on this side are also performing a protective role.

Somerset is fortunate in having a number of distinctive and very impressive church towers built in the fifteenth and early sixteenth centuries. At this time the county had grown rich on the profits of the woollen cloth trade and money was available to build fine structures, most of which are to be found in West Somerset.

Many of these towers incorporate a collection of large and distinctive Hunky Punk figures, situated high up on the towers and projecting far out from the structure, to break up straight sections of masonry. During this period of tower building, small teams of masons were employed, each team having a master carver responsible for producing features such as the Hunky Punks which are carved in an expressive, free-hand way unlike some other elements such as tracery, mullions and columns which were more often produced by less experienced stone carvers using templates. The details for heraldic figures would have been followed precisely from specific requirements in the builder's contract, but the choice of design for Hunky Punk figures was probably usually left to the imagination of the carvers and work on these figures was carried out during the winter months within the comfort of the stone carver's workshop. It is unlikely that there was direct religious supervision of the carver during this work and very few of these figures appear to be based on religious themes.

A wide range of subjects appear, including birds, animals, a few human figures, one devil and various heraldic animals. Mythical subjects are represented by such creatures as the griffin, which has the head, wings and front feet of an eagle and the rear quarters of a lion; an unusual cockatrice with the head and front legs of a cockerel and rear quarters of a

*A Hunky Punk dragon on St Mary
the Virgin church, Isle Abbots.*

A Hunky Punk dragon in the form of a sea serpent on St Mary's church, Bishops Lydeard.

lion, rather than the more usual rear end of a serpent or dragon. Dragons vary in details, but none of these carvings seem to possess the long tail that generally characterizes a dragon. This may well have been because of the difficulty experienced in portraying them on carvings to be mounted on a wall.

In some of these examples the rear quarters of the dragons, without long tails, look more like those of lions. In most cases the mouth is open to display teeth or sometimes a protruding tongue. In three cases the dragon is clearly shown with a stone in its mouth, a design probably inspired by the legend of the dragon killed at Kingston St Mary by a stone rolled into its mouth (see p. 85).

Many of these dragons have necks drawn back to strike, presenting a frightening and fierce aspect. The angle of the neck causes the chest of the creatures to be puffed out, in some cases to a quite an extreme degree. The surface treatment of the bodies, best seen on the chests, varies from an almost feather like patterning which is probably meant to be scales, to a smooth finish while an example of a ribbed chest is to be seen at East Lyng.

This tradition of carving dragon figures on towers persisted for a long time, as when the tower of St John the Baptist, Carhampton, was rebuilt in 1870, three large and very fearsome gargoyle dragons were placed on the tower looking out over the marshes where St Carantoc had his encounter with a dragon, a well known story at the time.

Even the relatively plain church of St Andrew in Taunton, built in 1880, has a dragon carving on it, although this saint is not generally associated with dragons, (however, see the story of The Devil's Dragon of Wiveliscombe, (p. 101), so its presence just seems to be following a long Somerset tradition of placing protective dragons on church buildings that still seems to persist. In the year 2000 inner doors were added to the entrance of St Barnabas's church, Queen Camel, and the door handles were made in the form of stylised dragons!

The following are good examples of Hunky Punk dragon carvings on fifteenth- and sixteenth-century Somerset church towers:

Church	Location
Brent Knoll, St Michael's	West face (dragon eating a man)
Bishops Lydeard, St Mary's	NW corner (sea serpent) S centre (sea serpent) W centre (sea serpent) SW corner (dragon, stone in mouth)
Isle Abbots, St Mary the Virgin	E centre (dragon with pointed teeth) S centre (dragon with protruding tongue. SE corner (dragon, stone in mouth) W centre (dragon with pointed teeth)
East Lyng, St Bartholomew's	N right (dragon, stone in mouth) E left (dragon, badly weathered) E right (dragon with ribbed chest) W right (dragon, head damaged)
North Petherton, St Mary's	SE corner (dragon, flattened teeth) SW corner (dragon, pointed teeth)

11

Miscellaneous Dragons

In a county so rich in dragon lore, and where the interest in dragons has persisted so long, it is not surprising to find representations of dragons in forms other than the ones already dealt with. These appear in all kinds of locations and range from carvings on church fonts to ornamental cast iron railings. A wide range of these are detailed in this section with examples from the eleventh to the twentieth centuries. This is not a complete list and the diligent dragon hunter will be able to discover more examples around Somerset.

Dragon Inns

Many inns and public houses have a long history and their original names usually relate to local people, legends and events and provide a useful link with early local history. It was made a legal requirement in England by Richard II in 1393 that inns had to display a sign of some emblem or figure that easily identified them as a place where ale was brewed and sold. Dragons were common on early inn signs and many of these would probably have featured a wyvern, only later being replaced by a four-legged dragon, as this form 'evolved'. There was a 'Sign of the Cockatrice' in London in 1608, and a 'Wiverne' was also to be found in the seventeenth century. The use of the dragon as an inn sign inspired John Taylor to write in 1636:

> These Dragons onely bite and sting all such,
> And doe immod'ratly haunt them too much:
> But those that use them well, from them shall find
> joy to the Heart, and comfort to the minde.

An examination of dragon names used for public houses throughout the county of Somerset shows that there is a geographical grouping that ties up with the area of the county where other 'dragon evidence' such as ancient church carvings and legends are to be found. In two cases, that

The sign of The Green Dragon Inn, South Street, Wellington.

at Bilbrook and the former inn at Dinder, there is a direct link with a dragon story, while the George and Pilgrim Hotel at Glastonbury commemorates a legendary visit this dragon slaying saint was supposed to have made to the town.

Somerset has a large number of 'dragon inns' compared to other counties today. Once again this shows a significant pattern, as the greater the number of dragon legends to be found in a county, then the larger the number of 'dragon inns' that are to be found (see Appendix 2). John Taylor in his *Travels Through London to Visit all the Taverns* (1636) lists all the inns in London, at a time when there were hundreds of them, and records only seven named The Green Dragon. There are currently seven central London pubs with a dragon name compared to twenty-eight in Somerset.

The George Hotel at Nunney, Somerset, which features St George on horseback painted on its front wall as its inn sign, may have some connection with the medieval St George painting in the local church, although this is dedicated to All Saints. The George and Dragon was a popular subject for inn signs and one is even mentioned in Shakespear's *King John* (1590), 'St George that swindg'd the dragon, and e'er since sits on his horse back at mine hostess' door'.

A Somerset pub, The Ring of Bells in St James Street, Taunton, has no known local associations with dragons but manages to feature them by including the image of a dragon on the hand bells shown on its sign. The Hobby Horse, a public house at Minehead, is named after the creature that can be interpreted as having its origins not in a horse but a dragon! (see p. 165)

Dragon Inns of Somerset and Bristol

Dragons
The Dragon House Hotel, Bilbrook (formerly The Green Dragon)
The Dragon and Wheel, Dinder (no longer a pub)
The Green Dragon, Friarn Street, Bridgwater
The Green Dragon, Badmington Road, Bristol
The Green Dragon Inn, Combe St Nicholas
The Green Dragon Inn, South Street, Wellington
The Green Dragon, St Michael's Avenue, Yeovil

St George and the Dragon
The George and Dragon, London Road, Batheaston, Bath
The George and Dragon, Church Road, Redfield, Bristol
The George and Dragon, Stanshalls Road, Felton
The George and Dragon, High Street, Pensford
The George and Dragon, Winterbourne Hill

St George
The George Inn, Manor Road, Abbots Leigh
The George Inn, Mill Lane, Bathampton, Bath
The George Inn, Wells Road, Bristol
The George Inn, Brompton Regis
The George Inn, Croscombe, Shepton Mallet
The George Inn, Gurney Slade
The George Inn, Glastonbury
The George Inn, Church Street, Martock
The George Inn, Main Road, Middlezoy
The George Inn, High Street, Norton St Phillip
The George Inn, High Street, Shirehampton
The George Inn, Mill Street, Wincanton
The George Hotel, St Mary Street, Nether Stowey
The George, Nunney

Dragon related
The Hobby Horse Inn, The Esplanade, Minehead

Bridgwater's Gable Dragon

The River Parrett formed a boundary between the Saxon's to the east and the Britons to the west after the victory of King Cenwalh of Wessex in 658. The town that later grew up on the river seems to have become a major Saxon settlement, and developed as a port from Norman times. Bridgwater was formerly a borough and once a busy port because of its position at the head of the Parrett estuary, and today it is still a sizable town, now famed for its impressive carnival held each year. A fine dragon is to be found on the roof of a building in the Somerset Brick and Tile Museum, East Quay, Bridgwater. This dragon is made of red terracotta, fierce looking and typical of many 'modern' dragons featuring an elongated angular face, prominent ears, sharp teeth, four legs and a long tail. It was made as a gable end finial in the late nineteenth or early twentieth century and was used as a decorative feature on Victorian or Edwardian buildings. While this example has a purely decorative function it may have been inspired by the pottery dragon figures, known as *Chih-wen*, which were placed on the roofs of houses and temples in China to protect the building from lightning and fire.

St Mary's church in Bridgwater has a number of Hunky Punk dragons on its exterior. While not unusual in Somerset, these are either found on the tower, as protective talismans on the porch, or are to be found on the north side of the church. However, in the case of St Mary's these classic

The terracotta gable end dragon, Bridgwater.

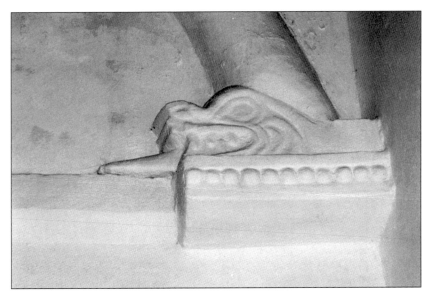

A Norman dragon's head, St Mary's Church, Christon.

dragons, with bat-like wings, are to be found on a ledge on all sides of the building.

Christon's Supportive Dragons

Christon, a small village to the south east of Weston-super-Mare has a small Norman church dedicated to St Mary. It was built in about 1170, but there are signs of Anglo-Saxon masonry to be seen in the exterior walls of the chancel, dating from around 1060-80. It has a very impressive late Norman door arch and a nave rebuilt in the fifteenth century.

The dragons are to be found in the under tower just before the chancel. The arches are twelfth century and there are plain, heavily rounded ribs running upwards from each corner, and each of the ribs is 'supported' on a dragon's head in profile. Each head has a large and prominent eye, an elongated mouth with sharp teeth and a long, blunt protruding tongue. The definition of the four heads varies as they have been covered in layers of lime wash over the centuries and it is possible that they were originally painted in colours.

The Dinder Dragons and The Linton Worm

Dinder, a small village lying on the River Sheppy, lies to the east of Wells, set in a valley, its name means 'the house in the valley'. The church,

A Norman Amphisbaena dragon, St Michael's church, Dinder.

dedicated to St Michael, lies behind Dinder House, and is in the Perpendicular style (1374–1550). However, the dragon carving is Norman and is a survival from an earlier building. It was taken down during the Cromwellian period, broken and thrown into the undercroft, where it was discovered by the Victorians and placed in its present position. Other dragons can be found around the church: in a niche above the porch can be seen a nice stone carving showing St Michael slaying a dragon; while another dragon can be found in the lych gate, the covered entrance to the churchyard.

The Dinder dragon is an Amphisbaena, a dragon with a head at both ends. In this case it is a serpent-style dragon with each head having an elongated face with well-carved features, and a 'dog tooth and ball' pattern on its body linking the two heads. It is now situated above the south chancel, window but originally it probably formed part of a Norman entrance doorway to the earlier church.

On the side of the lych gate can be found a brass monument to Arthur Fownes Somerville (1850–1942). This incorporates the crest of the Somerville family which features a wyvern above a wheel, all done in enamel, and the use of this device on their crest commemorates the brave deed of one of their dragon slaying ancestors, John Somerville who killed the Linton Worm in 1174 (see opposite). Linton is in Roxburgh, Scotland and this is traditionally where the battle took place between the Great Linton Worm and John Somerville, but there is a Somerset connection that can still be seen in the county today.

At Dinder, is a former inn, now a private house, and on this building is the old sign of the Dragon and Wheel Inn. A curious name if the story it represents is not known. So why did a Somerset inn name and sign commemorate an early medieval dragon battle that took place in Scotland? The answer lies in the ownership of the local manor. The manor passed through various hands and was owned by the de Rodney family until the mid-seventeenth century when it was sold to Richard Hicks. It passed down in this family, until the mid-eighteenth century when one of the Hicks family heiresses married George Somerville (died 1776), a descendent of the dragon slayer of Linton. The story obviously appealed to the locals, particularly the inn keeper who decided to feature it as his sign. There can be little doubt the locals were aware of the story, even though it originated so far away, or the sign and name would have made no sense to them.

John Somerville, a historical character and knighted, allegedly, for his bravery in killing a dragon was given the post of Royal Falconer and created first Baron of Linton. The Somervilles bore a dragon in the form of a wyvern on their crest and in Linton church there is a carving that shows a man with a falcon on his arm fighting a dragon. The story is probably another example of a 'charter myth', where a family claimed they got their titles and lands due to the bravery of a dragon-killing ancestor.

The Tale of the Linton Worm

There was a great worm at Linton, that was so large it could coil itself round Worm Hill three times. It ravaged the district, causing great damage, but was finally killed by John Somerville in 1174. John took a long lance and asked the villagers if they had any pitch. They replied that they had and he then told them to boil it up in a pot, and when it had melted he added boiling resin and brimstone. He took a great piece of peat and dipped it into the boiling mixture and then fixed a wheel to the tip of his lance and tied the peat, now impregnated with the mixture, to it and rode out to find the monster carrying this strange weapon. (The idea of the wheel was probably to prevent the peat being pushed back up the lance when he thrust it at the dragon.)

When he came near the dragon he allowed the smoke and fumes from the glowing peat to blow into the face of the monster which drew in its breath, choking on the fumes. So great was its agony that when it wrapped its tail around a hill it left indentations that can still be seen today. John Somerville rode up close to the dragon, which could no longer see properly, and thrust the burning peat down its throat and held it there until the monster was dead.

The sign of the former Dragon and Wheel Inn, Dinder.

It is of interest that there is another Scottish story of a dragon killing of this type, this one by Hector Gunn from Sutherland. It is possible that the inspiration for these tales originated from a passage in the Old Testament that was lost from the Bible at the Reformation when it was removed from the authorized version. In this Daniel, now better known for his adventures with lions, claimed that the dragon the King of Babylon worshipped was merely a brass statue:

And the King said unto Daniel, 'Wilt thou say that this is of brass? Lo, he liveth, and eateth and drinketh; thou canst not say that he is no living god: therefore, worship you him! ' Then said Daniel 'I will worship the Lord my god. For he is a living god. But give me these, O King, and I shall slay this dragon without a sword or staff '. The King then said, ' I give thee these '. Then Daniel took pitch, and fat, and hair and did seethe them together, and made lumps thereof: this he put in the dragon's mouth, so the dragon did eat and burst asunder: and Daniel said 'Lo! These are the gods ye worship'.

The Flax Bourton St Michael's Dragons

The village lies on the A370 between Bristol and Weston-super-Mare and the church, which is dedicated to St Michael, has a fine and very ornate Norman doorway, above which is a carving of St Michael and the dragon and inside is another interesting dragon carving.

The St Michael carving is naively executed but very striking and dates from the eleventh century. It depicts St Michael wearing a toga-like garment, with wings extended, standing upon the body of a dragon and looking down on his defeated enemy. The saint has an upraised sword in his right hand and a staff, topped with a cross, in his left. The base of the saint's staff is thrust into the open mouth of the winged dragon which is lying on its back, its long tailed curled round on itself. A series of raised dots run along the side of the tail and its body as far as the neck.

Inside the church is a Norman chancel arch with an interesting carving of a flying serpent (worm) on one of its capitals. This dragon has no legs, but a long snake-like body and a tail ending in a trefoil, a pair of bird-like wings and a large mouth with sharp teeth. On the same capital are two serpents that have zig-zag bodies but no wings.

The Gaulden Manor Chinese Dragon

Gaulden Manor is located in the hamlet of Tolland off the A358 to the west of Taunton. Parts of the building are believed to date from the

An eleventh-century carving of St Michael and the dragon, St Michael's church, Flax Bourton.

A Norman carving of a winged, flying serpent at St Michael's church, Flax Bourton.

twelfth century, and it was originally part of a priory until it came into private ownership on the dissolution of the monasteries in 1539. It has passed though several hands since then and is noted for its fine plaster-work dating from 1642. The manor is open to the public at certain times. On the roof of the building can be found a Chinese dragon, placed there by a former owner, Mr Lowther in about 1950. He had spent some time in China and brought it back on his return to England. The Chinese dragon is quite different from the Western dragon in many respects. Dragons in China play no part in creation myths and are generally benev-olent creatures, usually helping mankind, unlike the monsters that 'terrorized' medieval Britain and Europe.

There are four types of dragon in Chinese folklore and both sexes are represented. All are long lived, taking three thousand years to reach maturity. They were believed to have a strong influence on the weather and therefore were responsible for bringing rain to help crops grow, while violent thunder storms were caused by a pair of dragons fighting in the air, the lightning being heavenly fire sent to put a stop to the fight. Dragons fighting in water caused floods and there were also 'earth' dragons, some of which guarded treasure.

As Chinese dragons were basically good creatures, they did not get slain as in the west, but parts of their bodies were in demand as potent medicines. A medical work by the Emperor Shen Nung (2,838–2,698 BC) strongly advocates their properties. Dragon bones (fossilized dinosaur bones) were sold in pharmacies until quite recently. As in tradition they were not killed and were also regarded as near immortal, it is not clear how body parts of dragons became available! As with British dragons, some have taken on a protective role and it is for this reason that images of dragons, *Chih-wen*, such as the one at Gaulden Manor, were placed on the rooftops to ward off fire or lightning strikes.

The Gaulden Manor dragon is made of bronze and is about two feet (60 cm) long. It is beautifully cast and of a typical Chinese design, with its tail looped back.

The Glastonbury St Georges

The church of St John the Baptist at Glastonbury is probably built on the site of St Aldhelm's monastery, but appeared to have no monastic status by the time of the Norman conquest. The church has been rebuilt and altered a number of times in its long history, probably undergoing a complete rebuild in the twelfth century, again during the fifteenth century and a more recent and controversial restoration between 1852 and 1866.

The south porch of the church was built in 1428 and a second story was added to it in 1484. In a niche on the right hand side of the upper story is a large carving of St George and the dragon. This is a slightly

A Chinese bronze roof dragon, used in China to ward off lightning strikes and protect from fire, now in use at Gauldon Manor.

unusual depiction as the saint is standing on the dragon and seems to be holding it down with a long shafted cross rather than transfixing it with a lance or about to strike it with his sword, which is a more familiar way of depicting the story.

In the south transept is St George's chapel which has a parclose screen separating the chapel from the rest of the church on which is depicted St George killing the dragon. The carving, within a roundel, shows the saint in medieval armour mounted on a horse and attacking a dragon which cowers beneath the horse, but with upturned head and open mouth. The parclose screen was re-erected in the church by the architect Bligh Bond in 1927. It had been split up and built into houses used by church wardens during the medieval period.

In the chapel of St George is a fine stained glass window made in 1924 by Danielli. This is notable as it shows the whole St George story, spread over three windows. Most stained glass windows just show the saint and the dragon, but in this example St George is shown in the central window impaling a fearsome green dragon with a spear; his magnificent white horse appears in both this and the left hand window. The princess

A fifteenth-century St George and the dragon on the porch of St John the Baptist church, Glastonbury.

A stained-glass window showing the story of St George rescuing the princess from the dragon, St John the Baptist church, Glastonbury.

A parish chest, bought in 1421, bearing the arms of St George in the centre, flanked by the arms of the Earl of Devon (left) and the Earl of Salisbury (right) in St John the Baptist church, Glastonbury.

143

rescued by St George is shown in the right hand window, where she kneels with a guardian angel above her. In the left hand window can be seen a castle with the King and Queen standing on a balcony watching the rescue of their daughter.

The church has a parish chest, bought in 1421 to hold the church records, which bears the arms of St George in the centre, flanked by those of the Earl of Devon (three balls) and the Earl of Salisbury (three lozenges).

The church also possesses an alms dish, believed to date from the early sixteenth century, which also shows the saint. It appears to have been made in the Netherlands.

On the Danielli stained glass window, just above the St George window, can also be seen an image of St Michael (plate XXIII). While many stained glass windows and other images of this saint and the defeated dragon can be found, this one is a very notable example as it shows a very unusual type of dragon. Instead of being a reptilian beast this one takes the form of a green humanoid angel, naked with green, scaly skin, a pair of small horns on its head, and with wings like those of a bat. All these characteristics show it should be classified as a Hominoida Chlorodraco ('human-like green dragon'). The dragon crouches and reaches up to take hold of a pan of the scales being used by St Michael to weigh the souls he has pulled from hell to see if they are worthy of being saved, in an attempt to pull them back into the underworld.

The Isle Abbots Dragons

Isle Abbots is located north of Ilminster, its name arising from the fact it stands near the River Isle, and was owned by the Abbey of Muchelney from the Saxon times until the Dissolution of the monasteries. The village has a regular layout suggesting an early planned settlement and contains a variety of buildings dating from the medieval period to the eighteenth century.

The church of St Mary the Virgin is located at the east end of the village, and has a thirteenth-century chancel and a four-stage tower built in the fifteenth century. The church is notably rich in dragon images, both inside and out, but then this village was always an isolated one on the edge of extensive and mysterious marshlands!

Three fine Hunky Punk dragons can be seen on the tower but other dragon carvings can be found on the exterior of the building along with two dragon-fighting saints.

As in a few other churches in the county, a dragon is to be found guarding each corner of the medieval porch. Both are in fine condition, the one on the left having a stone in its mouth, while that on the right has a long protruding tongue and puffed out chest so common in this type of Somerset carving.

On the north side of the fifteenth-century tower is a fine carving of St Michael standing above a dragon that has its head and neck raised and through which the saint has thrust his spear so hard it is protruding from the other side. On the opposite side of the tower is a carving, a little weathered, that shows St George sitting on a horse above a dragon that has its head turned towards him, revealing sharp teeth.

Other dragon images are to be found carved on the font, which is of a square-shaped design and bears Norman decorations but may be of Saxon origin. On the North side of the font is a dragon shown upside down, with a pattern of flowing lines behind it. There are two theories accounting for it being on its back – it may represent pagan or non Christian beliefs that have been 'reversed' by baptism; or it may be that this was the first of the four carvings to be executed and was done while the bowl was inverted and so may in fact be a mistake.

On the West side are two indeterminate designs in recesses, followed by four inset arched niches. The first of these contains an anvil with a

A fifteenth-century representation of St Michael fighting the dragon on the tower of St Mary the Virgin church, Isle Abbots.

A Norman carving of an apparently unique scorpion-tailed dragon on the west side of the font, St Mary the Virgin church, Isle Abbots.

sword standing upright upon it; the second and third contain a unique type of dragon, facing left, with one of its two feet raised against the edge of the niche, while its body passes behind the upright of the two niches. Its tail is raised and terminates in a scorpion-like stinging tip. The final niche is occupied by a fleur de lys. These images, difficult to photograph, can be seen in a line drawing on page 27.

Interpretation of this sequence of images is difficult. In some stories a dragon slayer had a special sword, or other weapon, made with which to defeat the monster (for example, Siegfred) and the sword and anvil may depict this, but iron was also believed to have the power to resist or combat evil in all its forms so perhaps these items simply represent 'iron'.

This scorpion-tailed dragon is apparently unique, and as such there is no standard name for it, so 'Arachnidraco' (from *Arachnida* the group to which scorpions belong, and *drakon* – the Greek word for dragon), would seem to be an appropriate description. During the medieval period, and probably from the time of the crusades in the twelfth century, the scorpion was used to represent either jealousy or treachery, and this may be its meaning here. The fleur de lys may have no particular significance beyond a decorative device to fill the final niche.

On the south side of the font is a panel in which the central part is occupied by a stylized plant, probably meant to represent a tree, and to the left of it is a dragon. Further curling, plant-like designs occupy the space at each end of the panel. The creature in this scene has sometimes been interpreted as being a dove, but it also resembles a wyvern, which would make it a representation of the Tree of Life and Dragon as found in many other Norman church carvings. These are particularly common on the tympanum above the main door into buildings (see p. 9 and 10).

The church contains a number of interesting kneelers or hassocks embroidered in recent years by ladies in the village. The designs are inspired by aspects of village life and symbols of the saints featured on the church tower, and one bears a representation of a fire breathing dragon (plate XVI).

The Lullington Fighting Cockatrice

Lullington lies to the north of Frome and the name is derived from 'settlement of Lulla's people'. It is a pretty village with a pleasing grouping of buildings. Before the Norman Conquest the manor belonged to King Harold who was killed at the Battle of Hastings. The church, dedicated to All Saints, is Norman dating from the late eleventh century. Above one doorway is an interesting carving of a griffin and another beast consuming the Tree of Life. In other parts of Britain such Tree of Life carvings above doorways have dragons eating the tree, but the only Somerset example of a Tree of Life and dragon appears on the font at Isle Abbots, described above.

Among the carvings to be found on a late eleventh-century arch in the church is a pair of fighting cockatrices. Both creatures adopt the attitude of fighting cocks and one of them seems to be getting the upper hand. This is a particularly fine and early representation of this fairly rare type of dragon and is also unusual because the dragons are depicted fighting (plate XV).

The Nunney St George

Nunney is a delightful little village just south west of Frome on the eastern edge of the county. Its name probably derives from 'Nunna's Island'. All Saints church has a thirteenth-century chancel rebuilt in 1874, aisles and transepts of the fourteenth century and a south porch and tower dating from around 1500. Inside the church can be found a Norman font and the remains of a wall painting of St George, that most famous of all dragon slayers. This painting, approximately four feet (1.2 m) high, dates from the fifteenth century and is to be found above the north arcade of the nave. It had been hidden under layers of paint and plaster for many years and was uncovered in the early twentieth century.

The image is rather fragmentary. St George is depicted on foot, wearing period armour with a cross on it. He holds a spear that he is thrusting into the body of a dragon, although this section of the painting is damaged so it is difficult to make out any details of the creature, the background to the scene is red. The colours, while somewhat faded, are still quite clear.

In the chancel is a memorial tablet to the Revd William Powell Davies who was rector from 1898 to 1911 and died in 1931. The tablet features his family coat of arms with a 'cross flory' and a 'dragon rampant' on the shield, and another, a 'dragon statant' on the crest that appears above the shield. As his name suggests, the Revd Davies was of Welsh origin, so the dragon on the crest is the red dragon of Wales and the motto on the coat of arms is in Welsh.

The dragon in Wales, in both legend and as a symbol, has its own interesting story and another Red Dragon of Wales can be found in Somerset on the inn sign of the Dragon House Hotel on the A358 Taunton to Minehead road.

A fifteenth-century painting of St George in battle with the dragon, All Saints church, Nunney.

Memorial to the Revd William Powel Davies, whose coat of arms incorporates two dragons, All Saints church, Nunney. The one on the crest is a Welsh dragon.

In Church Street, Nunney, is the George Hotel, which features a painting of St George on a rearing horse as its sign on the front wall.

The Queen Camel Dragons

The attractive village of Queen Camel lies south west of Sparkford on the A359 to Yeovil. Many of its houses date from the same period following a large fire in 1634 which destroyed seventy buildings. The fourteenth-century church of St Barnabas is in the centre of the village and includes some fine features including a number of dragons. The oldest representations are to be found on the roof bosses and date from the fourteenth century. There are thirty-five bosses, three of which depict dragons and each of these shows a different type of monster.

The first of these depicts a large, winged dragon and a tree with birds in it or around it. The dragon is on the right, has a very menacing attitude, and looks towards the tree on the left, but one bird has left its safe perch and can be seen below the dragon's head. This scene is another representation from the early medieval Bestiary illustrating the legend of Peridexion, also to be seen on a bench end at Hatch Beauchamp. (see p. 113)

A second roof boss bears an Amphisbaena dragon. In this version of the double headed dragon the creature is shown with wings and a second head upon its tail which curves round and upwards. The body is covered in large

149

A font cover featuring four magnificent sea serpents. St Barnabas church, Queen Camel.

scales. Since the head and tail of these creatures were so alike it was supposed, in popular legend, to be able to move either forwards or backwards with equal ease and was used to represent something particularly sinister.

The third dragon roof boss shows a Cockatrice, with the head and comb of a cock, bat-like wings and a scaly body that ends in a serpent's or lizard's tail. The most dangerous of all dragons.

The font cover is a magnificent oak feature bearing four sea serpents. This was made to commemorate John Gare (1867-1934) and his wife Louisa (1872-1945). It bears an inscription from the Bible: 'In my name shall they cast out devils; they shall speak with new tongues, they shall take up serpents.'

To complete the Queen Camel church's assemblage of dragon images is a pair of door handles, on the inner glass doors to the porch, made to commemorate the Second Millennium. They take the form of multi-coloured Celtic or Saxon-style dragons, reminiscent of those found on enamelled jewellery of that period (plate XVII).

The St Decuman's Dragons

St Decuman's church is located to the south west of the town of Watchet on the Somerset coast. St Decuman was a sixth-century saint who was martyred here and whose shrine was moved to the site of the present church in the eleventh century. The chancel is late thirteenth century but the rest of the building dates from around 1500.

On the exterior of the church can be seen three very fine dragons with bat-like wings and curved tails. These are arranged at intervals along a ledge on the opposite side of the building to the porch. They all look over their shoulders at the observer on the ground and have a very wide-eyed and almost surprised expression on their faces.

Inside the church is a fine medieval carving of St George and the dragon about one foot (30 cm) tall. This is carved into a niche on the column just behind the pulpit. The saint stands in full armour above the dragon, with a spear, now missing its point, ready to be thrust into the monster (plate XXII).

Taunton's Many Dragons

As might be expected in the principle town of a county whose coat of arms is a dragon, a number of these creatures are to be found in various forms. Dragons are also represented in a number of companies' logos and trade marks of some local organisations and services. These use the Wyvern, the early form of two-legged dragon used on the battle standards of the West Saxons but these 'wyverns' sometimes appear with four legs so are really heraldic dragons!

The oldest dragon in Taunton is the wyvern on the coat of arms of Henry VII (1485-1509) at Taunton Castle.

The only dragon on St Andrew's church, Taunton.

A fine dragon carving on the former Leper Hospital, Taunton.

Representations of the wyvern and four-legged dragons can be seen in a number of forms from a period covering five hundred years of Taunton's history.

Taunton Castle, now occupied by the county museum, was built in 1138 and is located just off the main shopping centre, near to the bus station. Above the gate house of the inner ward is a carved stone bearing the coat of arms of Henry VII (1485 - 1509). It is now somewhat weathered, but one of the supporters can be quite clearly seen to be a wyvern.

The impressive tower of St Mary Magdalen's church (163 feet) was originally built in 1488–1514 but was completely rebuilt, in faithful replica, in 1858–62 after the original was found to be unsafe. On the tower can be seen a large carved figure of St George, unmounted, and battling with the dragon. The carving has suffered some damage to one of the arms and the spear St George is using to kill the dragon.

Inside the church are some very fine stained glass windows. Two, both on the same wall of the nave, depict St George. One, dedicated to Robert Blackall Montgomery, late Colonel to the Somersetshire Regiment who died in 1884, shows St George holding a shield with a red cross and a red rose in each quarter, standing above a defeated green dragon. The second window, dedicated to the soldiers of the West Somerset Yeomanry and the Somerset Light Infantry who were killed in the First World War shows the saint standing triumphant above a large red dragon.

The dragon railings outside County Hall, Taunton.

A wyvern on a mosaic in Magdalene Lane, Taunton.

St Andrew's church stands at the junction of Kingston Road and Greenway Avenue to the north of Taunton town centre. The church was built in 1880 at a cost of £2,500 by H.J. Spiller after the design of J. Houghton Spencer, both of Taunton. It has a very nicely carved dragon on the end of the building fronting Kingston Road. It is to be found at the end of an ornamental ledge, which it appears to be biting, and is the only dragon on this relatively plain church.

The original Somerset College of Art, a stone building in the neo-classical style in Corporation Street near to the bus station, was built in 1907 to a design by C. Sampson and A.B. Cottam. It is now occupied by the Social Services Department. The building bears a magnificent coat of arms carved in stone and flanked by the figures of a painter and a sculptor. As it predates the official granting of a coat of arms by the College of Heralds the shield bears not only the Wessex dragon (without a mace), but also a crown and a winged angel's head, a device also to be found in other parts of the town.

County Hall is located to the south of the town in The Crescent and was built in 1935 by the architect E. Vincent Harris. Three dragons can be found here in various forms. Above the main entrance is a very fine stone carving of the county arms, featuring a dragon on a shield flanked by cherubs and wheat sheaves (plate XVIII).

An interesting interpretation of a dragon is to be seen on the cast iron railings each side of the main entrance, where they form the uprights while hanging inside the entrance of County Hall are a pair of very fine tapestries, each about six feet (2 m) high. One of these depicts the red dragon of Somerset along with some of the animals and plants associated

A terracotta dragon made by Philip Thompson, County Library, Taunton.

The Somerset dragon on a lamp post, Taunton.

155

The sign on the Dragon Tea Rooms, Taunton.

A mural featuring dragons on the side of the swimming pool, Taunton, painted by local children on a workshop course run at the local theatre in about 1994.

with the county (plate XIX and cover). These were made by the renowned textile artist Candice Bahowth using wool and natural dyes. They were commissioned by the council to commemorate the centenary of the County Council in 1989 and each took six months to make.

St Margaret's Leper Hospital, probably founded by Taunton Priory at the beginning of the twelfth century but rebuilt about 1510–15 by Richard Bere, Abbot of Glastonbury, was used as an almshouse from 1612 to 1938. It was then occupied by the Somerset Guild of Craftsmen and the Somerset Rural Community Council but has remained derelict following two arson attacks that destroyed the thatched roof. On the front wall is a fine stone carving showing a Wessex dragon above a curling ribbon bearing the motto: 'Sumorsaete Ealle'. The words 'Rebuilt 1939' appear in raised lettering below the ribbon.

In Magdalene Lane, just off East Reach, can be found a wyvern in the form of a coloured mosaic, that measures about seven by eight feet and is set into the pavement in front of the Wyvern Blinds shop. At one end of the lane is a modern Perspex sign, showing the shops to be found in the lane, which bears a prominent representation of a wyvern.

On the front of the library building in Paul Street is a superb dragon just over five feet (1.5 m) in diameter made of cream terracotta using locally dug clay. This was made in 1996 by the artist Philip Thompson who has also created works for the Houses of Parliament, Windsor Castle, Westminster Abbey and Wells Cathedral.

Taunton lamp posts, particularly in 'sensitive locations' such as conservation areas, are sometimes of a more traditional form in cast iron and bear a dragon silhouette near their base, most of which are painted in gold or silver.

In The Crescent, near County Hall, are to be found The Dragon Tea Rooms, in a building that was formerly the Dragon Book Shop, with a well-painted sign on the side of the building.

On the side of the swimming baths in St James Street is to be seen, at present, a large mural featuring dragons painted by children during a workshop session at the local Brewhouse Theatre in about 1994.

The Trull Dragon Slayers

The parish church of All Saints at Trull, a village to the south west of Taunton, was served by the monks of Taunton Priory till 1308 when it came under the care of the vicar of St Mary's, Taunton. The tower, which is quite plain compared to many others, was built at the end of the thirteenth century, but the rest of the building dates from the fifteenth

St George on a fifteenth-century stained-glass window in All Saints church, Trull.

century. One of the most notable items is the beautifully carved and undamaged wooden pulpit of around 1500 but of interest to the dragon hunter is a stained glass window. Regarded by this church as one of its greatest treasure's is some late fifteenth-century stained glass in the south window of the chancel. This depicts three dragon slaying saints, George (above), Margaret and Michael, along with their foes (plate XXIII). All three dragons are golden yellow and those of St George and St Margaret have small spikes on both body and tail.

The Dragons of Wells Cathedral

Tradition says that a minster church was first founded at Wells by Ine, King of the West Saxons around 705 and, following much rebuilding and enlargement became what is now regarded as one of England's finest cathedrals. The dragon hunter will find a number of carved stone dragons among the cathedrals rich collection of carving both inside and outside the building, on stained glass and on embroideries, particularly the hanging behind the Bishop's throne. The most notable and impressive dragons are to be found on the cathedral's misericords.

To relieve the strain on the legs of the clergy during the long services, wooden seats were hinged with a ledge projecting at right angles on the edge, so that when the seat was raised the vicar or chorister could rest his weight on this ledge, while still giving the appearance of standing up. Hence the name misericord which means 'act of mercy'.

The underside of each of these ledges is carved with a range of figures or small scenes featuring humans or animals. The misericords at Wells, each carved from a single piece of oak, are regarded as the best examples in England and date from about 1339. Sixty-nine of the original ninety survive, and of these, seven feature superb representations of dragons involved in a variety of situations and activities.

Unfortunately, the carvings on the Wells misericords can only be examined by appointment, but photographs of all of them appear in a cathedral publication, (see bibliography). There is another example of a misericord dragon, but less fine, dating from 1499-1516, in St Martin's church, Worle.

The Wells misericord carvings are numbered and the dragon interest ones are as follows:

12. Two wyverns with wings and prominent ears are depicted biting their own tails, (Ouroboros) and represent eternity or eternal life. These two creatures are entwined together.

14. In this scene a wyvern is shown sinking its teeth into the chest of a horse that is, in turn, biting the wing of the dragon.

24. A man is shown fighting a wyvern that has bird-like wings. He appears to be about to cut off its head with a sword that he has already positioned below the dragon's jaws.

30. This seat depicts a dragon apparently asleep, squatting down on its two legs but with wings extended. It has been suggested that this may be a young or baby dragon.

40. A wyvern with a fearsome head and a long neck is shown apparently biting or preening its own bird-like wings.

42. This carving, which is unfinished, shows two dragons with bat-like wings apparently fighting each other.

61. This is a very fine and animated carving of a dragon being slain. The monster, with bat-like wings, a long curling tail and sharp claws is carved with great skill to show its ribs and the folds of its skin where its neck is curved. The dragon slayer is depicted covering the eyes of the monster with his right hand and thrusting a spear, held in his left hand, down its throat through its partly opened mouth.

On the staircase leading to the Chapter House, from around 1260, are two carved corbels of interest. One shows a monk or priest with a crutch under his left arm, the end of which rests in the mouth of a dragon coiled at his feet. The second carving, on the opposite side of the staircase to the first, shows a layman wearing good quality clothing, who also has a crutch under his arm, the end of which rests in the mouth of a coiled dragon. Possibly these dragons represent the Devil and the disabilities the punishment meted out, to both clergy and the laity, for failing to follow the true path of God. Disability and illness were believed in medieval times to be punishment for sins committed.

In the Chapter House undercroft is another carving on a roof boss, from about 1260, that has a similar theme. In this case there are two human heads with a dragon biting the head of each person. Possible interpretations of this include dragons representing evil thoughts entering the minds of the people, or possibly they represent madness as both human figures have 'odd' looks on their faces. Alternatively, it may represent illnesses where coloured lights may be experienced, such as a

A thirteenth-century carving on the stairs to the Chapter House at Wells Cathedral using dragons to symbolize disability.

A thirteenth-century boss in the undercroft of Wells Cathedral showing dragons biting the heads of two figures, perhaps symbolizing mental illness or 'evil thoughts'.

migraine headache. A similar carving, on a typhinium, with beasts biting a head can be found in St Margret's church, Queen Charlton.

On each side of the interior of the cathedral's north porch are four elongated dragons of varying designs. It is not unusual to find dragon carvings on the north side of churches as this is the direction from which 'evil' was said to come. On a corbel near the entrance to the stairs to the Chapter House, can be seen a carving that is sometimes described as a salamander. However, it has the characteristic appearance of a crocodile, as perceived by the medieval mind. Early portrayals of the crocodile have acted as the inspiration for many later artists impressions of dragons.

The church of St Cuthbert in Wells, with its 122 (37 m) feet high tower, appears to be fifteenth century from the outside but has thirteenth-century arcade pillars and other early features inside. Its dedication suggests the church is of Saxon origin and it was for a long time the city church where the mayor and corporation worshipped and one of whose church wardens were appointed by the corporation.

Bronze statuette of St George on a war memorial outside St Cuthbert's church, Wells.

A very impressive war memorial, erected just after the First World War, is to be found in the churchyard. This consists of a tall stone column carved in the medieval style, the head of which contains four niches, each of which is occupied by a bronze statuette of a different saint. One of these is a fine representation of St George standing above the defeated dragon.

West Bagborough's Rood Dragons

This village is situated on the southern slope of the Quantocks, its name derived either from 'Bacga's Hill' or 'Badger's Hill'. The church, which is dedicated to St Pancras, the only one with this dedication in Somerset, lies outside the main village and close to Bagborough House. It now looks quite isolated, but it is thought that village settlement was once grouped round the church but was deserted at some stage, perhaps due to a plague. The church is mostly of the fifteenth century, with an earlier tower and font, but had a north aisle added in 1839 and underwent a lot of restoration in the nineteenth century. Most of the interior woodwork

A stained-glass window showing St Michael fighting a seven-headed dragon, St Pancras church, West Bagborough. He has already cut off two of the heads!

is 'modern', designed by Sir Ninian Comper, with the exception of some sixteenth century bench ends.

The Rood is the figure of Christ crucified, flanked by St Mary and St John, which is raised above the rood screen. Most churches once contained this image, but most were removed during the Reformation or during the Cromwellian period. This example, by Sir Ninian Comper, is on a beam across the chancel arch where the rood screen once stood, and acts as a war memorial to the men of the village who fell in the First World War. The figures of St Mary and St John are each supported on the heads of dragons, with green bodies and scales picked out in gold and red tongues protruding from open mouths with pointed teeth. Their tails are curled around and each touches the base of the cross as if they are holding it upright. The design may possibly illustrate a passage from the Gospel of St John (3: 8–9) where John writes of Jesus referring to the Nehushtan or brazen serpent held up by Moses in the desert to save his people from a plague of serpents – 'And as Moses lifted up the serpent in the wilderness, even so must the Son of man be lifted up: that whosoever believeth in him should not perish, but have eternal life.'

The incident Jesus refers to is found in The Book of Numbers (29:8–9) and reads – 'And the Lord said unto Moses, make thee a fiery serpent, and set it upon a standard: and it shall come to pass, that everyone that is bitten, when he seeth it shall live'. The fiery serpent here could actually refer to a dragon rather than a snake.

A stained glass window, dated 1930, in the northern aisle shows St Michael with sword and shield battling a blue, seven-headed dragon. Five heads are intact, two stumps can be seen and one detached head is visible. A seven-headed dragon is mentioned in the Book of the Revelation of St John (Revelations 12:3) but is there described as red.

One of the stained glass windows in the south wall of the chancel contains a roundel within a rope border, showing St George, with sword and shield, standing above a red dragon with a long curling tail.

The Wootton Courtney St George

This village, between Minehead and Dunkery Beacon, derives its name from 'settlement in the wood' and the 'Courtney' element from the de Courtney family who held the manor in the thirteenth century. The church, dedicated to All Saints, has a thirteenth century west tower but mainly fifteenth century construction with nineteenth century restorations. The north aisle has a fine series of carved bosses, two of which feature dragons. It is difficult to make out details unless the light is good, but close up photographs of them are displayed in the church.

One boss has a very spirited carving of St George who is mounted on horse back and is impaling a wyvern, a two-legged dragon having wings with overturned edges. The saints long lance is thrust into the mouth of the dragon, which has gripped the foreleg of the horse in its claw and wrapped its tail firmly round its hind leg in its death throes.

Anotherboss depicts a wyvern which, like the dragon on the St George boss has distinctive wings one with an overturned edge, the other being erect. It has a series of large scales running down the back of its neck, along its back and onto its thick and stubby tail. Its head is turned away from the observer and towards the ceiling.

12

The (Dinehead Sailor's Horse

– A (Disunderstood Dragon

There are still ceremonies held around Britain featuring 'hobby horses', animal effigies worn by a person in the parade, usually slung from the shoulders and moved in a way to suggest the movement of the animal concerned. Hobby dragons, sheep and other animals are known to have been used in the past and until the mid-nineteenth century many such ceremonies were held, of which only a few still occur today. Most of these events occur in midwinter and have obvious pagan fertility overtones. There are, however, two 'hobby horses' that still appear in ceremonies today and are worth closer examination as they have features that make them different from others. These are the 'Minehead Sailor's Horse' (plate XXIV) and the 'Padstow old 'oss' which appears each year at Padstow in Cornwall. Both of these have features in common with each other but which differentiate them from other 'hobby horses'.

Both the Minehead and Padstow 'horses' make their appearance on May Day, not in mid-winter or Easter, like other hobby horses. They are geographically isolated from other such ceremonies and are constructed in a different way to hobby horses used in other parts of the country. Also they do not traditionally behave like horses when they are in their parades and do not actually look like one. So it was suggested by Jacqueline Simpson (*British Dragons,* 1980) that they might originally have been something else – dragons!

Both of these 'horses' parade through the streets accompanied by musicians collecting money from the onlookers, both are grotesque figures having no real resemblance to a horse (particularly the one from Minehead), both stage mock 'attacks' on the watching crowd and in former times both were considerably more 'aggressive' in their display than they are today.

The 'Padstow old 'oss', whose body is a black cloth hanging from a six feet (1.8 m) wide circular frame balanced on the shoulders of the operator, chases girls and tries to catch them under the cloth which, in the old days, was also smeared with blacking.

The Minehead Sailor's Horse, whose ancestor may have been a dragon, is lifted off its 'operator'.

The 'Minehead Sailor's Horse' is about eight feet (2.4 m) long and also worn on the shoulders of the operator. The hangings on the side are of canvas, sometimes painted with large circles, which may be significant as a number of dragon representations from the medieval period onwards show roundels on their wings. In more recent times it also has the words 'Sailor's Horse' painted on it in large letters, the whole body having a curious curved shape at the front and back. The upper part of the body is hung with scraps of ribbons, cloth, velvet and silk. At the back it once had a cow's tail decorated with ribbons, with which its attendants attempted to trap bystanders and, until about 1880, its head, covered in hare skin, had snapping jaws, used to bite those who would not pay up! Since that time the 'Horse' has lost its head! The man who carries the costume wears a tall, conical hat, the exact design varying from year to year.

The Minehead Sailor's 'Horse' used to be accompanied by masked attendants called Gullivers, who would hit people with a boot if they refused to give the 'Horse' money. Today it is accompanied by musicians, one of whom plays a drum which dates back to the seventeenth century. The 'booting' still takes place, carried out on the third night at Cher Steep where victims are caught in the street and booted ten times by a blow from the front of the 'horse'. The victim is held by the attendants who are today called 'the crew'. Both 'horses' give much pleasure and excitement by their mock aggressive, but notably unhorse-like, behaviour.

One anecdote from Minehead says that the port was once threatened by Viking raiders and to deter them some local fishermen disguised a boat to look like a sea dragon and took it out to sea. This frightened the Norsemen who sailed away again, so the coastal villages were saved and the Minehead 'Horse' was supposed to represent this disguised boat. The 'Horse' does not resemble a sea dragon, but it does not resemble a horse either.

There are other clues that suggest that this creature was originally a dragon. Minehead is only four miles (6.4 km) from Carhampton where a fearsome dragon was quelled by Carantoc, the Celtic saint (see p. 77), while Padstow has St Petroc who is also associated with dragon stories (see p. 43).

During its procession the Minehead 'Horse' traditionally visits Dunster Castle in the course of its rounds and this castle is where St Carantoc led his dragon.

An account written in the 1880s shows how important this procession was in the past, and gives further clues to its origin.

On the evening of 30 April the 'Horse', accompanied by a drum went to White Cross where his attendants danced round him. This was called the Warning Night. [Today the 'Horse' still parades around the town accompanied by a drum and sometimes other musical instruments.] At 6 a.m. on May Morning it again went out to White Cross where the 'Horse' performed a dance accompanied by many people. The prettiest girl present was chosen as May Queen. In even earlier times a May King was also chosen and the pair were 'married'. The Queen was lifted onto the 'Horse' who carried her round on his back. Later in the morning the 'Horse' and its entourage appeared in the streets of Minehead when the 'Horse' attacked the bystanders. They then set off for the traditional visit to Dunster Castle where the Luttrell family, owners of the castle, received them with honour, regaling them with beer and victuals. On 2 May it again appeared and went from the Quay to Alcombe. On 3 May the ceremonies ended with the 'Horse' visiting yet another cross roads, this time at Cher Steep.

This is much the same routine that is still performed today.

The legend of St Carantoc would have been well known in the medieval period, so could this be the last remnant of a religious festival? A clue to this is in the fact that the procession takes place on May Day. The feast day of St Carantoc is the 16 May, so if the ceremony was originally held on that day and was either being secularised or held unofficially despite prohibition, as happened in the case of many traditional folk festivals during the seventeenth century, it may have been incorporated in the May Day festivities. These the church never really managed to completely suppress. Unfortunately there are no church or other records surviving to show how the people of Minehead, Carhampton and the region celebrated the feast day of St Carantoc in the medieval period.

Another notable feature of the older descriptions is that while there is a suggested fertility aspect in the marriage of the May Queen and the May King, as is usual in May Day ceremonies, there was nothing in the behaviour of the Minehead 'Horse' to suggest fertility aspects or symbolism that may represent death and revival. However, some of the behaviour of the Padstow 'Horse' can be interpreted this way, as it occasionally dips and then raises its body (the Minehead 'Horse' has recently also adopted this dipping behaviour).

So while the origins of both the 'Padstow old 'oss' and the 'Minehead Sailor's Horse' can only be based on surmise, there does appear to be some evidence that both started life as fearsome dragons a few hundred years ago.

Appendix 1

The Gurt Vurm of Shervage Wood
in the Somerset Dialect

This was given, in dialect, by Ruth Tongue in *Somerset Folklore,* 1965. She recalled the story being told to her when she was a little girl by a jovial storyteller from the village of Nether Stowey.

Now, look see, I wad'n there then so I couldn' swear 'twas the truth, could I now? But 'twas like this, see –

There was a tremenjus gurt vurm up-over in Shervage Wood. Ah – all a-lyin' in and out the trees an' round about the Camp, so big and fat round as two-three girt oaks. When her felt hungry her just up'n swallow down 'bout six or sebm ponies or sheep and went to sleep comfortable.

Well then, by 'n by, farmers do notice sheep idn' upalong an' there wadn' more'n a capful of skinny old ponies for Bridgwater Fair that year. Where was t'others gone to, then?

Arter a shepherd an' a couple of Stowey broom-squires went upalong to look-see and didn' come back neither there wadn' nobody at all ready to go pickin' worts on the hill when Triscombe Revel time come around next year.

The vurm he were gettin' a bit short on his meals like. The deer an' the rabbits they was all over to Hurley Beacon t'other side of the hills, and there wadn' a sheep left, and the ponies, I reckon, had run down over valley to Forty Acre.

Now, I did hear there were a poor old soul who sold the worts for Triscombe Revel. Her made they tarts beautivull and filled'n up with a thick dap o' cream that made 'ee come back for more so fast as a dog'll eat whitpot.

Well, look see, there wadn' likely to be no tarts for her to sell on account of no one going up over to see how worts was ripenin', n' if her didn' sell no tarts to Triscombe Revel her'd get no money for the rent. Poor old soul! Her was in a shrammle!

Well then, there come a stranger to Crowcombe, all the way from Stogumber I expect, and he were a woodman looking for work. So her up'n tells'n, "Why don't 'ee try cuttin' in Shervage Wood upover, and look-see if worts is getting ripe?" Poor old soul were desperate, see. So her give'n a cider firkin and bread 'n cheese, and watches'n go off up combe.

Being a Stogumber stranger he wadn' used to Quantock Hills and by the time he'd a - walked into Shervage Wood and seed a wonderful fine lot of worts on the way he were feeling 'twere quite time for his cider.

So he looks round like and he seed a bit of a girt log in the fern. So down he quots an' takes a swig from the firkin an' gets out his bread 'n cheese. He'd just got nicely started on his nummet when the log begins to squirmy about under'n.

"Holt a bit!" says he, picking up his axe, "Thee do movey do thee? Take that, then." 'And the axe came down so hard on the log he cutt'n in two— Mind, I'm only telling 'ee what 'tis said — and both the ends of the log begun to bleed !

Then the one end it up and run as hard as it could go to Bilbrook, and t'other end it runned to Kingston St Mary, and since they two halves went the wrong way to meet, the gurt vurm couldn' nowise grow together again – so her died.

Folks down to Bilbrook they call their place Dragon Cross, and folk to Kingston St Mary they boasts about the same old tale of a fiery dragon – might be as they got the head end of our gurt vurm – but he were all Quantock to start with!

Well then, the woodman he just sat and finished his nummet, and cut his faggot, and took the poor old soul a girt hatful of worts. "There were a dragon there fust go off," he tells her very thoughtful. But all her says is, "Didn' 'ee know? Didn' someone tell 'ee? Her were a Crowcombe woman.".

Appendix 2

Comparison of the 'Dragon Inns' of Somerset with other counties

	Green Dragon	George & Dragon	George & Wheel	The Dragon Horse	The Hobby or Dragon's Head	The Dragon Head	Total of Inns'	Total of known dragon stories
Somerset	6	5	17	1	0	0	28	14
Cornwall	0	1	2	0	0	0	3	3
Glos	1	0	3	0	0	0	4	2
London (central)	0	2	4	0	0	1	7	0
Shrops, Heref'd & Mid-Wales	3	2	2	0	0	0	7	8
South Wales	2	0	4	0	0	1	7	3
Surrey	1	0	3	0	0	0	4	1
Yorkshire	1	6	6	0	0	1	14	11

Appendix 3

For many centuries the men of the West Country went to war under the banner of a dragon, both Celts and later Saxons. This dragon symbolism was still alive in the Second World War, when the 43rd Wessex Division, chose the Wessex dragon as their emblem.

This was a four-clawed wyvern, its mouth open to show a protruding arrow-like tongue. The upper part of its body was scaled, while the lower part had ring scales, and it stood with one of its feet raised in the position described heraldically as *wyvern passant*, an unusual stance for this creature.

H. J. Channon wrote a Ballard about this division in 1945 where he uses dragon imagery, not only seeing the 'Wessex Dragon' beating the enemy, but by bringing in allusions to 'the men of Siegfried's line'. Siegfried, in Teutonic mythology, fought the dragon Fafnir using a technique that might have been regarded as 'unsporting' by a British dragon slayer and also nearly suffered the treachery of his 'partner' in the slaying! (see Appendix 4).

The Dragon of Wessex
A Ballad of 'The Fighting Yellow Devils'

On Senlac ridge the Wessex Dragon breathed Its last,
No many-headed serpent like the hydra!
Henceforth, the fate of England was to be a vassal state.
So thought the fierce and martial Bishop Odo,
He who at Hastings struck no gentle blows with mace,
And slew Leofwine, brother of the Saxon King.
The Bayeux tapestry survives; the clever hands,
That deftly worked the scenes portrayed,
the Dragon gored and crushed, without a spark of life.

The wyvern used as the emblem of the 43rd Wessex Division during the Second World War.

Almost nine hundred years had passed,

Since Norman William massed his mighty force,

To span the Channel's narrow sea-marge blue.

And once again the island's fate was in the balance.

The Prussion brutish hordes with hatred gazed,

Upon the Kentish shore.

To Huns in Normandy the colourful embroidered fabric
gave wild joy.

What once had been achieved could well be done again,

But the spirit of Drake breathed upon the waters.

And Nelson from his column in Trafalgar square,

Looked down with countenance benign,

As if to say: 'Fear not these braggadoclos'.

Huns laughed to scorn the saviour of our land,
Who promised nought but 'blood and toil, and tears and sweat',
Before the road to victory was in sight.
In gloating mood they never ceased to boast
That if on continental shores the Allies tried to land,
Not one would long survive. The men of Siegfried's line
would see to that.
A bloody sacrifice to Odin was in store,
(These bestial Nazis, breed of wicked Locki,
Contriver of all evil. Odin would have scorned).

As for dragons bred in Wessex shires,
The German Demogorgon would make short work of them.
Heels clicked in Caen, and swastika were kept in store.
One day to be unfurled in London's public parks.
Such arrogance now reaps what it has sown,
Rabshakeh spoke, but we were not confounded or dismayed.

O'er Hunnish realms a blast descends,
And they who took the sword now fall by it in their own land.
Extremity of suffering is indispensable,
If German people are to learn to hate,
That militarism which for so long
They have idealized and idolized.

Then D-Day came, the Golden Dragon leapt ashore at
Courseulles,
The men of Wessex wore its yellow flash,
Who were these paladins?
Whence this fine breed of hero's born to face the direst crisis
Our Island ever knew?
Unnurtured in the arts of war.

They came from every trade and occupation,
Policemen, lawyers, shopkeepers and tillers of the soil.
Apprentices and schoolboys in their thousands,
Lads of heedless daring and stubborn fortitude.

They said: "This is our finest hour", and so it was,
For when the brazen throat of war has ceased to roar.
It will be told of these tough warriors from the West
That never has their valour been surpassed.

In Normandy their record was superbly fine.
The River Orne could not prevent the Dragon's onward rush,
On Hill 112 the German's from its sting recoiled,
A glorious achievement this, for SS troops were there,
And they had made the hill into a mighty bastion.
The 43rd had won their spurs, and from the enemy they got
The sobriquet 'The Fighting Yellow Devils'.
The next assault required a powerful heave at no small cost,
Before the Panzer wolfpack fled in terror dread,
Down wooded slopes of dominating Mont Picon.

The chance to make a great drive north had come,
At Vernon where the Seine was reached.
The Golden Dragon took a fearsome leap,
And on the eastern bank a footing firmly made.
All honour to the Wessex Royal Engineers.
Grand work they did against immeasurable odds,
Through the bridgehead the British armoured units poured,
And so the liberation of Brussels and Antwerp was achieved.
In fight fine fettle was the Dragon of the West,
In vain the Huns tried hard to clip its claws,
The more they tried, the more they felt its deadly maul.

From gaping jaws belched bursts of devastating flame,
Squelching the squealing vulpine foe in full retreat.
The Wessex men gave him no chance to get his second wind.
Good hunting they wanted, good hunting they got.
No time to gather roses, fresh and fair, in Picardy,
But time to think of England, and her simple pleasures,
Of village greens where sixers climbed the summer sky,
Of fishing in the Brue, and cup ties, and cosy beds,
Of lovely cottage gardens with Wisterias in bloom,

And, most of all, of wives and kiddies back in England dear.
Into Holland irresistibly advanced the infantry,
The 43rd leading ahead, so near but yet so far,
A big prize lay, the northern gateway into Germany.
At Grave on reedy Maas, the Dragon jumped again.
Round Nijmegan the Wessex men performed prodigious feats
This name their much emblazoned shield will surely bear.
Ten miles up north the illustrious Arnhem hero's,
On Nether Rhine had won immortal fame.

Another Homer will that stirring epic write,
Three thousand from the toils of death came back,
Saved by friends who wore the yellow Wyvern flash.
The gallantry of that small band who crossed the Lak,
To reach the hard pressed airborne garrison,
Is the supreme example of the immortal words:
'Greater love hath no man than this,
That a man lay down his life for his friends'.
In all our island's story has been no page grander than this,
Men rose to heights of heroism superb.

The Dragon lay crouching for another leap,
A well-deserved pause, and than a fitting climax to their work –
'The Fighting Yellow Devil's' were the British van.
In Niederhelde, the first Reich village that fell to British troops,
No joyful welcome here!
The greatest test of stamina was now to come,
A battle waged with floods, and snow and slush.
These Lionhearts, with a smile today, and a song tomorrow,
Won through, and their endurance showed,
They would have graced the company of Shackleton and Scott.

Then Runstedt gambled on a final fling and lost.
The Dragon stood on watchful guard at bridgeheads on the Meuse.
Ils ne passeront pas. The Dragon would have kept its vow.
Back in the line, its fangs did deadly work
At Geilenkirchen, Cleve and Goch.

The fighting had been grim, and tough the opposition,
Before the 43rd rolled up the powerful German defences.

Fritz Klaffke and his fellow cocky Panzer Grenadiers,
Berserkers they thought themselves to be,
Were pummelled, thumped and beaten up.
In savage fighting which, in farmhouse ruins,
Took the form of cut-and-thrust, and fisticuffs,
And hefty hand-offs to the jaws, until Fritz cried: "Craven".
The gunners too, kept up a killing pace,
Their 25 pounders firing at a range of fourteen hundred yards.

In Xanten, native town of Siegfried, seized by Wessex men,
Who talks of dragon-slayers, mighty as of old?
Some sycophantic fraus emerge from frowsy cellars,
And if the ghost of Siegfred haunts the place,
Disconsolently it must view the sickly scene.
As tokens of surrender flutter in the breeze,
The Wehrmacht were to hold at any price
This town that hinged the powerful Wesel barrier line.
Hitler proposes, but Monty disposes. That happened once again.
For shells came off the pitch so devilish fast
that in the ring of fire and steel no Hun could live.

Winston Churchill has crossed the Rhine.
A great symbolic act! Supremely fitting too, that he
The man of vision whose faith in Britain's darkest hour
Upheld us in those fateful summer days of ninety forty,
Should cross the Rhine to drive as nail in the Fuehrer's coffin.
For this is Britain's hour, the hour for which,
We long have striven through *blood, toil, tears and sweat.*
Be sure the men of Wessex did not 'miss the boat',
By walloping the Panzer Grenadiers along the Lower Rhine
These hardy veterans did much to make the crossing possible.

The Allies now pursue their almost unimpeded course,
Along the German autobahns.

But the dragon has a spot of work to do first on the left,
Where fanatical Huns resist our progress to the V-2 coast.
Invincibly the Dragon pushes on with speedy liberation of
Holland as the goal.
The dykes have saved our gallant Dutch friends in the past.
This time, we hope, West Country lads will come as
their deliverers.

Out of the shadow of night, the world is rolling into light,
except in Hunland, where twilight ushers in stygian darkness.
Where is the Nero of the North?
His strident voice is hushed.
He made the sorrows of mankind his sport.
Apothesis was his dream; he wears a crown of infamy instead.
Where are the slavish Nibelungs of Silesia and the Ruhr?
Barbarossa still sleeps, so the cry of werewolf is raised.
Its nothing new that Nazis are by nature wolves.

Ichabod!, Ichabod! The glory is departed from Hitler's realms.
The sword of Damocles hangs threateningly above the German folk.
The Reich, that was to last a thousand years,
Collapses like a castle made of sand.
The Cyanean Rocks are closing on the beaten wehrmacht
And though circuitous and obscure the feet of Nemesis how sure!

The Bayeux tapestry will need an extra length,
On which the jaunty Golden Dragon, rampant after all its triumphs
Proudly will appear, the field stained red
With blood of very gallant Wessex men.
In hateful fray they deemed far more
At stake than Empire gained or lost.
They fought to guard eternal values,
And the precious things and common joys of life,
Freedom from fear, freedom to think,
Freedom to enjoy the love of liberty and truth,
And all that makes life worth the living.

The state was made for man, not man for the state.
Real-politik has had its day, and must cease to be.
These hero's fought and died that one and all
Of every race, creed, tongue and colour
Might live in peace, and homes secure,
Free to call their personality their own,
Not subject to one inexorable will.
Splendid Hearts, who made the World rarer gifts than gold,
For you the trumpets have sounded on the other side.
Let's see to it that we are worthy of their sovereign sacrifice,
And that their valour was not unavailing.

Appendix 4

Siegfried's fight with the Dragon Fafnir

The story of Siegfried's fight with a dragon appears in the *Nibelungenlied* Saga and is forever immortalized in Richard Wagner's opera-cycle *The Ring*. An almost identical story, whose hero is Sigurd, is found in the Norse *Volsungasaga*.

The imagery was used by H.J. Channon in his ballad about the men of Wessex fighting the Germans in the Second World War, where he refers to the enemy as the 'men of Siegfried's line' (Appendix 3). He may also be alluding to the way Siegfried used deception to defeat the dragon, although the use of trickery is not unknown among British dragon slayers! There are a number of variations in this story in both Teutonic and Scandinavian mythology.

The Tale of Siegfried and Fafnir

Fafnir was the son of Hreidmar and, some say, was a giant. He had spent years gloating over his share of the treasure that he had got from Loki, and which he had acquired by killing his own father. Gradually he had taken on the form of a great dragon, one of the rightful guardian's of treasure. He lived on Gnitaheid, which means 'the Glittering Heath'. In order to destroy the dragon Fafnir, Siegfried asked Regin, Fafnir's brother, to make him a sword strong enough to defeat the dragon. Regin forged a sword and gave it to Siegfried, who tried out its strength by striking the anvil with it, but it immediately shattered.

So Regin began to forge a second and even better sword. When this was completed Siegfried again tested it by striking the anvil, but once again the sword shattered. So Siegfried then went to his mother and obtained his fathers sword which had been broken and from this Regin forged a third sword and gave it to Siegfried. Once again Siegfried tested its strength by striking it against the anvil, but this time it proved to be so strong that the blow cut the anvil in half. However, at the same time it was so sharp that it was able to cut in two a skein of wool that floated on a stream nearby. This sword was called Ridill.

Now Siegfried and Regin, went up to the moors, to the track along which Fafnir used to crawl when he went to drink, and the crag upon which he lay when he drank was said to be thirty fathoms (180 ft/54 m) high. When he saw this Siegfried said 'You told me that this monster was no bigger than any serpent, but his tracks look very big to me'. 'Dig a pit', said Regin, 'and sit in it, and when the dragon comes crawling along the track to the water, stab him in the heart and so you will destroy him'.

So Siegfried went up to the moors, but Regin went off, being very afraid. Then Siegfried dug a deep pit in which to conceal himself and other pits besides in which the monsters blood could run. And when the dragon Fafnir crawled down the track to drink from the water, the ground shook and the earth shuddered. The dragon breathed out a great cloud of poison all over the path ahead but Siegfried was neither frightened or dismayed.

When the dragon crawled across his pit, Siegfried thrust his sword into the left shoulder of Fafnir and it sank in up to its hilt. Then Siegfried leaped out of the pit, wrenching back his sword and stuck it into the heart of the monster, getting his arms bloody right up to his shoulder. When the dragon felt its death wound, it lashed its tail and its head, shattering everything that got in its way until finally Fafnir died.

Then Siegfried cut out the dragon's heart with his sword at the urging of Regin, who asked him to roast it so he could eat it. This he did, but when Siegfried tested the meat with his fingers to see if it was cooked he burnt himself and put his fingers in his mouth to cool them, but in so doing the blood from the dragon touched his tongue and he suddenly found he had gained the power to understand the language of birds. One of the carrion birds, attracted to the site by the body of the dragon, told Siegfried that Regin intended to kill him so he could keep Fanfir's treasure all for himself. The bird then advised Siegfried to eat the dragon's heart himself and drink of its blood.

So Siegfried took the sword with which he had slain Fafnir and killed Regin. He then ate the dragon's heart and drank some of his blood. When he examined the dragon's treasure, he found among all the golden items the *Aegishjalmur* – the Helm of Awe, *Andvaranaut* – the magic ring and the Haberk of Gold.

Appendix 5

Places in Britain with Dragon Legends

England

CHESHIRE: Middlewich, Moston.

COUNTY DURHAM: Durham, Lambton Castle (near Chester-le-Street), Sockburn, Bishop Auckland.

CORNWALL: Helston, Lewannick, Padstow.

CUMBERLAND: Renwick.

DERBYSHIRE: Baslow, Drakelow, Winlatter Rock, Wormhill in Millers Dale.

DEVON: Cadbury Castle/Dolbury Hill, Challacombe, Manaton, Winkleigh.

DORSET: Poundsbury.

DURHAM: Bishop Auckland.

ESSEX: Henham, Hornden, St Osyth, Saffron Waldon, Wormingford.

GLOUCESTERSHIRE: Deerhurst, Stinchcombe.

HAMPSHIRE: Bisterne, Burley, Wherwell.

HEREFORD AND WORCESTER: Brinsop, Mordiford, Wormelow Tump.

HERTFORDSHIRE: Berkhampstead, Brent Pelham, St. Albans.

LINCOLNSHIRE: Anwick, Castle Carlton, Walmsgate.

NORFOLK: Ludham.

NORTHUMBERLAND: Bamburgh, Money Hill (on Gunnarton Fell), Longwitton.

OXFORDSHIRE: Chipping Norton, Dragonhoard (near Garsington), Dragon Hill (Vale of the White Horse, Uffington).

SHROPSHIRE: Old Field Barrows (near Bromfield).

STAFFORDSHIRE: Wendesbury.

SUFFOLK: Bures, Little Cornard.

SURREY: Buckland.

SUSSEX: Bignor Hill, Fittleworth, Horsham, Lyminster, St Leonard's Forest.

WESTMORLAND: Hayes Water.
Worcestershire: Drakelowe (near
Wolverley).

YORKSHIRE: Beckhole, Cowthorne,
Drake Howe (near Bilsdale), Filey
Brigg, Handale Priory (near
Lofthouse), Kellington, Loschy Hill,
Nunnington, Sexhow, Slingsby,
Tanfield, Well, Wortley.

Channel Isles

JERSEY: La Hougue Bie, (near Five
Oaks).

Wales

ANGLESEY: Penmynydd.

CLWYD: Cynwch Lake, Llanrhaeadr-
ym-Mochnant, Llyn-y-Gadair, Nant
Gwynant, Penmynydd.

DYFED: Castle Gwys, Newcastle
Emlyn, Trellech a'r Betws.

GLAMORGAN: Cardiff, Penllin Castle,
Penmark.

GWYNEDD: Betws-y-Coed, Llyn
Cynwch (near Dolgellau), Llyn-y-
Gader, Penmynydd.

POWYS: Llandeilo Graban.

Scotland

ARGYLSHIRE: Ben Vair.
Dumfries and Galloway: Dalry.

KIRKCUDBRIGHTSHIRE: Solway Firth.

ROXBURGHSHIRE: Linton.

SUTHERLAND: Cnoc-na-Cnoimh (in
Glen Cassley).

TAYSIDE: Strathmartin.

Orkney Islands

Shetland Islands

Fitful Head

Bibliography

Adshead, A. *The Flying Serpent of Henham* (*Essex Countryside,* Autumn, 1954).

Allen, J., Griffiths, J. *The Book of the Dragon* (1979).

Alford, F.W. *The Hobby Horse and Other Animal Masks* (1978).

Anderson, M.D. *Drama and Imagery in British Churches* (1963).

Anon. *Misericords of Wells Cathedral* (1975, reprinted 1998).

Anon. *The Wonderful Legend of the Lambton Worm* (*c.* 1875).

Barber, R., Riches, A. *A Dictionary of Fabulous Beasts*(1971).

Baring-Gould, S. *Lives of the Saints* (1914).

Bayley, H. *The Lost Language of Symbolism* (1912).

Benton, J.R. *The Medieval Menagerie* (1992).

Binyon, L. *The Flight of the Dragon* (1911).

Blackburne, H. and Bond, M. *The Romance of St George's Chapel, Windsor* (1971).

Boger, E. *Myths, Scenes and Worthies of Somerset* (1887).

Bose, H. C. du *The Dragon, Image and Demon,* 1886.

Boyle, J. *Historical Dragon Slayers* in *Animals in Folklore* (ed. Porter, J.R
    and Russell), WMS 32, 1978.

Bush, R. *Somerset Stories* (1990).

Bush, R. *Somerset - The Complete Guide* (1994).

Cambell, J.F. *The Celtic Dragon Myth* (1911).

Carus, P. *The History of the Devil and the Idea of Evil* (1900).

Cawte, E.C. *Ritual Animal Disguises* (1978).

Cherry, J. (ed.) *Mythological Beasts* (1995).

Clark, D., Reeder, P. *The Wantley Dragon* in *Northern Earth Mysteries* 33, 11-17 (1987).

Collins, A. *Symbolism of Animals and Birds in English Church Architecture* (1913).

Costello, P. *In Search of Lake Monsters* (1974).

Dennys, R. *The Heraldic Imagination* (1975).

Devlin, J.D. *The Mordiford Dragon* (1848, reprinted 1978).

Elliott Smith, G. *The Evolution of the Dragon* (1919).

Farmer, D.H. *The Oxford History of Saints* (1987).

Frazer, Sir J.G. *Folk-lore in the Old Testament* (1923).

Garnet, R. *In the Wake of the Sea - Serpents* (1968).

Gordon, E.O. *Saint George* (1907).

Gould, C. et al *The Dragon* (1977).

Gould, M.M. *Sea Serpents* (1886).

Gresswell, H.P. *The Land of Quantock* (1903).

Guillaume, Le Clerc de Normandie (trans. Druce G.G.) *The Bestiary* (1936).

Harper, C. *The Hughendon Dragon* (1985).

Harte, J. *Dragons of the Marches* in *Mercian Mysteries* 20, 1-7 (1994).

Hartland, E.S. *The Dragon of Deerhurst* in *The Antiquary* XXXVIII, 1-6 (1902).

Hartland, E.S. *The Legend of Perseus* (1896).

Heaney, S. *Beowulf - a new translation* (1999).

Heaword, R. *Snap the Dragon* in *Albion* 2, 12-23 (1978).

Heylin, P. *The Historie of St George of Cappadocia* (1659).

Higgins, T.W. *'John Aller'* in *Folklore* IV, 399-400 (1893).

Hogarth, P., Clery, V. *Dragons* (1979).

Hoult, J. *Dragons, their History and Symbolism* (1990).

Huxley, F. *The Dragon: Nature of Spirit, Spirit of Nature* (1979).

Jewitt, L. *The Dragon of Wantley and the Family of Moore* (1887).

Jones, S. *Legends of Somerset* (1984).

Ingersoll, E. *Dragons and Dragon Lore* (1928, reprinted 1968).

Lane, R. *Snap the Norwich Dragon* (1976).

Lawrence, B. *Somerset Legends* (1973).

Lofmark, C. *A History of the Red Dragon* (1995).

Lum, P.B. *Fabulous Beasts* (1952).

Lyons, A. *Essex Dragons* in *Essex Countryside*, (Summer 1956).

Manderville, Sir John *The Bodley Version of Mandervilles Travels* (1962).

Marcus, C.J. *St George of England* (1929).

Mathews, F.W. *Tales of the Blackdown Boarderland* (1923).

Metford, J.C.J. *Dictionary of Christian Lore and Legend* (1983).

Meurger, M. *Lake Monster Traditions: A Cross Cultral Analysis* (1988).

Montague-Smith, P.W. *The Royal Line of Succession* (1968).

Neale, J.M., Webb, B. (Ed) *Durandus, The Symbolism of Churches and Church Ornaments* (1843).

Newman, P. *The Hill of the Dragon* (1979).

Oldham, C.G. *The Sun and the Serpent* (1905).

Palmer, K. *The Folk Lore of Somerset* (1976).

Pennick, N. *Dragons of the West* (1997).

Pepler, H.D.C. *Concerning Dragons* (1916).

Pevsner, N. *The Buildings of England: North Somerset and Bristol* (1958).

Pevsner, N. *The Buildings of England: South and West Somerset* (1958).

Poole, C.H. *The Customs, Superstitions and Legends of Somerset* (1877, reprinted 1970).

Savage, A. (trans) *The Anglo-Saxon Chronicles* (2000).

Screeton, P. *The Lambton Worm and Other Northumbrian Dragon Legends* (1978).

Sharp, C. *The Worm of Lambton* (1830, reprinted in *The Bishoprick Garland*, 1834).

Simpson, J. *British Dragons* (1980).

Smith, G. E. *The Evolution of the Dragon* (1919).

Smithett Lewis, L. *Glastonbury–The Mother of Saints* (1927).

Somerville, C. *The Ballad of Bishop Jocelyn and the Dragon of Worminster Slight (2001)*.

Stuart, G.B. *The Dragon's Pool* in *Sussex County Magazine* VI, 154–56 (1932).

Sweeney, J.B. *A Pictorial History of Sea Monsters* (1972).

Tatham, Cannon *Dragon Folklore in Sussex* in *Sussex County Magazine* 5, 662 (19—).

Tatlock, J.S.P. *The Dragons of Wessex and Wales* in *Speculum* 8, 223–35 (1933).

Thompson, C.J.S. *The Mystery and Lore of Monsters* (1930).

Tongue, R. *Somerset Folklore* in *Folklore* VIII, 185–86 (1965).

Tongue, R. *Billy Biter and the Parkin* in *Folklore* LXXVIII, 139–41 (1969).

Tongue, R. *Forgotten Folk Tales of the English Counties* (1970).

Topsell, E. *The Historie of Foure-Footed Beastes, Serpents and Insects*
　　　(1608, r. Cass, W, 1967; Johnson, W.J., 1973)

Twigg, A. *The Red Dragon* (2000).

Visser, M.W. de. *The Dragon in China and Japan* (1913).

Ward, A.W., Waller, A.R. (ed.) *The Cambridge History of English Literature*, 1 (1933).

Waddell, H. *Beasts and Saints* (1934).

Webber, R. *The Devon and Somerset Blackdowns* (1976).

Whistler, C.W. *Local Traditions in the Quantocks* in *Folklore* XIX (1908).

White, T.H. *The Book of Beasts* (1969).

Whitlock, R. *Here be Dragons* (1983).

Wright, P.P. *Hunky Punks* (1982).

Wright, P.P. *The Rural Bench Ends of Somerset* (1983).

Acknowledgements

My thanks go to all those who have given help or advice during the course of this work:

David Bromwich, Ros Comer, Graham Daws, The Dean and Chapter of Wells Cathedral, Lt Col. Elliot, Joyce Halliday. Phillip Lancaster, Jean Moore, Dee Moxan, Terry Rookes, Mr and Mrs J. Starkie, Revd Peter Thorburn, Revd N.C. Venning, Valerie Wright, William J. Wych.

Index

Rhodes, dragon of 93
Romans 16, 45

S

Saint Carantoc 23, 30, 39,
41, 42, 77-80, 115,
130, 167, 168
Saint Decuman 150-51,
plate XXII
Saint Dubricius 39, 41,
42-43
Saint George 15, 35, 41,
45-50, 106-08, 111,
112, 116, 117, 122,
123, 132, 133, 141-44,
145, 147-48, 153, 158,
162, 164, plates I, IV,
XXI, XXII
Saint Margaret 50-52, 124,
158, plate XXIII
Saint Michael 13, 28, 41,
52-53, 101, 111, 115-
17, 136, 139, 144, 145,
158, 163, 164, plates
VI, XXIII
Saint Petroc 30, 41, 43-45,
113, 167
Saxons 32-33, 34, 35, 40,
63-64, 68, 71, 86
Scorpion 16, 27, 146
Sea dragon 29, 46-47,
119-21, 167
Sea serpents 18, 29, 150

Selwood, Abbot of
Glastonbury 49, 50, 118
Shervage Wood 23, 24, 69,
93-96, 169-70
Siegfried 172, 180-81
Somerville, Sir John 125,
137
Stoke-sub-Hamdon 30-36,
plate II

T

Taunton 56, 63, 130, 151-
57, plate XVIII, XIX
Thurloxton 69
Timberscombe 41
Tree of Life 10, 147
Trull 157-58, plate XXIII

U

Uther Pendragon 55, 68

V

Vale of the White Horse
35
Vikings 16, 69, 73

W

Warman, Simon 103, 123
Watchet 73
Wells 15, 16, 26, 28, 66,
69, 71, 96-101, 158-61